# DOVE RELEASE

First published 2010 by
Worple Press
PO Box 328
Tonbridge
Kent TN9 1WR

British Library Cataloguing in Publication data.
A catalogue record for this book is available from the British Library

ISBN 978 1 905208 13 5

Worple Press is an independent publisher specialising in poetry, art and
alternative titles. Worple Press can be contacted at:

Worple Press
PO Box 328
Tonbridge
Kent TN9 1WR

Tel:     01732  368958
E-mail:  theworpleco@aol.com
Website: www.worplepress.co.uk

Typeset and printed by Winstonmead Print, Loughborough, Leicestershire

# DOVE RELEASE

*New Flights and Voices*

edited and introduced by
David Morley

An ecologist and naturalist by background, David Morley's poetry has won fourteen writing awards and prizes including the Templar Poetry Prize, the Poetry Business Competition, an Arts Council of England Writer's Award, an Eric Gregory Award, the Raymond Williams Prize and a Hawthornden Fellowship. His previous collection *The Invisible Kings* was a Poetry Book Society Recommendation. David is also known for his pioneering ecological poetry installations within natural landscapes and the creation of 'slow poetry' sculptures and I-Cast poetry films. His 'writing challenges' podcasts are among the most popular literature downloads on iTunes worldwide: two episodes are now preloaded on to all demo Macs used in Apple Stores across the globe. He writes essays, criticism and reviews for *The Guardian* and *Poetry Review*.

Website: www.davidmorley.org.uk

*by the same writer*

**Poetry**
Releasing Stone
A Belfast Kiss
Mandelstam Variations
Clearing a Name
A Static Ballroom
Scientific Papers
Ludus Coventriae
The Invisible Kings
The Rose of the Moon
The Night of the Day
Enchantment

**Nonfiction**
Under the Rainbow: Writers and Artists in Schools
The Cambridge Introduction to Creative Writing

**Editor/co-editor**
Northern Stories 2
The New Poetry
Of Science
The Gift
Phoenix New Writing
No Longer Poetry: New Romanian Poets
Collected Poems of Geoffrey Holloway
The Greatest Gift
The Cambridge Companion to Creative Writing

**Film**
Gujarat Grand Mushairas

**Electronic Media**
Writing Challenges
Slow Poetry

# CONTENTS

# INTRODUCING
## *Dove Release*

I write a lot and am living all the time
And thinking about living. I loved to frequent you
After my teens and before my thirties.
You three together in a bar
I always preferred you because you were midmost
Most lustrous apparently strongest
Although now that I look back on you
What part have you played?

from 'To My Twenties', Kenneth Koch

*Dove Release* contains poems by over fifty writers, most of them poets in their twenties, including some winners of the Eric Gregory Awards. It also contains work by more senior poets. What unites them is a course at Warwick University called The Practice of Poetry. This course has taken place in many unusual spaces across the university including science departments and laboratories as well as art galleries and nature reserves.

Recently, students have written poems in and about the worlds of biology and physics thanks to a truly interdisciplinary project funded by The Capital Centre at Warwick called Science and Poetry. The poets worked alongside leading research scientists, and the scientists were charmed and challenged by their presence – and their questions - into fresh ways of thinking. The poets themselves were challenged and charmed by their experience of scientific knowledge and discovery.

I shall never forget the look of surprise and delight when Dr Andy Howes of Warwick's Centre for Magnetic Resonance made a magnet magically levitate before the eyes of these young poets, before leading them among a series of powerful magnets and explaining just what went on behind the lab's doors. Equally unforgettable was our visit to the School of Biological Sciences in which poetry students met with and interviewed a number of leading life scientists about their research – about their life's vocation. This sense of vocation - the sense of science becoming almost like an art form - was powerfully illustrated when as part of the Science and Poetry project the workshop took place in the centennial Charles Darwin exhibition in the Natural History Museum in London.

Over the past decade I've facilitated The Practice of Poetry for students at Warwick. I've always had an eye for the practical, ecological and scientific. I'm a former scientist – an ecologist. The natural world makes the poetry of this planet. For me, the study of natural history is one way of looking at the earth's poems. In negotiation with young poets, the poetry workshop evolved over years to reflect the ways we engage with the world.

I've always thought of an empty page as open space. Poets sometimes need to find open spaces in which to write, in which to ignite language and listen to the world. Writing is an act of community. Writing on your own is lonely but effective but writing in a group has advantages too, not least the *esprit de corps* that comes from being in a creative community. It's not just a question of company. *Where* we write affects how we write. A stanza is a room. Seminar rooms are fine, but you can't play many games in them nor listen to birds calling through birches.

The Practice of Poetry has been borrowing and inventing spaces for years. Art galleries, nature reserves, ancient woodland – all and more have supplied us with open spaces for creative discovery. The Writers' Room at Warwick University was invented and designed to provide artists and teachers with a room of their own, but it's a place from which to move outward as well as a place in which to soar inward.

And then there's teaching. It's important to hear more than one voice facilitating a workshop. Poetry teachers don't come for free, nor should they, so when I won a Warwick Award for Teaching Excellence, then a National Teaching Fellowship and, finally, project funding from The Capital Centre, I used the money to bring in poets from the world outside the academy to help me develop and deliver The Practice of Poetry.

These poets included Peter Blegvad, Zoë Brigley, Peter Carpenter, Jane Holland, Luke Kennard, Mimi Khalvati, Glyn Maxwell, Ruth Padel, Fiona Sampson and George Szirtes. Young poets such as Julia Forster, George Ttoouli and Andy Webb also made brilliant contributions. Although it's fair to say we had a lot of fun, our shared objective was serious as well as playful: how do we nurture the sensibilities and abilities of young poets so that they are of the world, so that we help them survive and thrive in the real world?

To address this objective, we decided that we needed to expand our understanding of the nature of poetry by not only expanding our use of practising poets but by also opening the gate of the course to scientists and natural philosophers. We hoped to foster among young poets a fresher understanding of poetry within the world, but one with a strong historical foundation across the two cultures. By increasing and subverting the spaces we used for the workshops we also hoped to open an understanding of poetry's relevance to other forms of knowledge including science and natural history.

Poetry is a vocation. Vocation is important to many professions, including those of science and medicine. In some ways I think this project fostered relationships of understanding between staff and students across the disciplines, especially with Biology and Physics. The vocation, craft and humour of scientists were all noted by our poets as they worked alongside them. It certainly challenged and changed some common preconceptions among poets about the world of science and creativity

Meeting scientists, and seeing live science, presented our poets with ideas, characters, and designs. It also gave us new language: the terminology of science is gravid with metaphor and is constantly inventing new terms for describing the stuff of life and the structures and shapes of the universe. What our poets were doing is ploughing a subject for language and material that they might use later in creative writing. They acted as ambassadors for creative thought and practice among students of science. They gained experience of people and ideas they otherwise may not have encountered.

This doesn't mean that *Dove Release* is a book of "science poems". It most certainly isn't. Some poets take science imagery and use it in innovative ways, sure, but *Dove Release* is principally an anthology of new poems by new poets – 'new flights and voices - not poems with a palpable design on readers. It's a representation of the work that came out of these workshops both during the project and in the years of development. For the sake of democratic presentation, the poets are presented in alphabetical order.

My thanks go to all the students who have shared my poetry workshops at Warwick University over the past years and to my fellow tutors: Peter Blegvad, Zoë Brigley, Peter Carpenter, Julia Forster, Jane Holland, Michael Hulse, Luke Kennard, Mimi Khalvati, Glyn Maxwell, Ruth Padel, Fiona Sampson, George Szirtes, George Ttoouli and Andy Webb. I would also like to thank Siobhan Keenan and Amanda Carpenter for their love and support.

This project was supported at first by a Warwick Award for Teaching Excellence, then a National Teaching Fellowship from the Higher Education Academy, and finally by project funding from The Capital Centre at the University of Warwick. The Science and Poetry project could not have happened without the support of Professor Carol Rutter, Dr Susan Brock, Dr Nick Monk and Helen Neal of The Capital Centre.

Students and tutors were made welcome by staff in several innovative working environments in order to make poems. I would like to thank Professor Robert Freedman and his fellow biologists at the School of Biological Sciences, Warwick University; Dr Andy Howes and the team at the Centre for Magnetic Resonance, Warwick University; and Sarah Shalgosky of The Mead Gallery. Thanks also to staff at: Tocil Woods Nature Reserve and Brandon Marsh Nature Reserve, both part of the Warwickshire Wildlife Trust; The Warwick Digital Laboratory; London Science Museum; Southbank Centre Poetry Library; Tate Modern; and the Darwin Exhibition at The Natural History Museum, London. David Morley, Warwick, October 2009

# ACKNOWLEDGEMENTS

Many thanks to the editors of print and online magazines, and pamphlets, in which some of these poems were previously published.

## The CAPITAL Centre
Creativity and Performance in Teaching and Learning

CAPITAL (Creativity and Performance in Teaching and Learning) Centre is a HEFCE-funded Centre for Excellence in Teaching and Learning at the University of Warwick.

# EVOLUTIONARY LINES

The mocking bird laughs then lays a theory before the eyes of mystery.
The mystery of mysteries, slowly and by little starts,
Begins the gaucho's life knowing fossil rocks the Kasbah.
Not only they, but wood so scared it speaks of ice,
Posing questions of saddle backed or domed.

The little old man was young once, no really.
He used to ride the giant tortoise despite issues of balance.
He followed the flutter of a gaudy butterfly
Allowing strange fruit to catch his eye.

Often cited but seldom read,
As most think naturalists are scared of clothes.
A monkey's uncle that bore a genius,
Son of Pan Troglodytes and his legendary smile.

The diary isn't legible, but holds tremendous style,
Talking more of grace than theory.
Most are ceratitina enough to touch the ammonite,
Including Geospiza fortis, whose bravery killed him.
At the front: bitis gabonica, a real hard nut.
At the back: merry chippus, careless as a shrug.

I turn to the Australopithecus afarensis,
Who doesn't know to surf or fear the water, swear or relate.
I'm nudged in the back by a Homo erectus,
Who is in turn unappreciated by Neanderthalensis.
I'm sure he bought me a drink last night and called me sapien.

I vary under domestication and spy a black and white photo of a zebra,
The MTV2 of the horse world,
Really just a fish that outgrew the sea.
Paranthropus robustus calls for a light,
His skull built like a tank, my hand begins to shake.

Some whales lie about being bears or frogs or human,
But they no longer have a leg to stand on.
To test them I sing a three-note chord,
And see if they differentiate the implausible from words.

*Toby Aisbitt*


## MY LOVE

She breathed a breath of don't fuck with me charm

Met lov ess fir har
Har ays har her
Har smayle har lov

*Toby Aisbitt*

# THE PAINTED LEOPARD

Any surrealist's pet
(they would muse at length
on the drooping aces; the first fat
drops of budding black
rained down upon
its flanks) – but always
Dalí's favourite: the ocelot.

How it would swipe
at that moustache, its own striped cheeks
*Vogue* war-paint;
*the op-art mine, of course*
as Salvador shakes his head
in disdain, reaching
for a napkin, sloshing more drink
into the gaping apple
of his mouth, dabbing at his chin.

While the ocelot, cradle-caught
under his arm, conducts a silent critique,
the restaurant negligently carved
open under its raptor gaze,
then discarded like a carcass
plucked clean, as it shifts,
muscle poured as if
from a cream jug
to fill out a shadowed pelt, outlandish
against a watered silk waistcoat.

Imagine its teeth gnawing,
bored of the thirties,
of Civil War;
its vanishing act at last
among the helpful trees
of Magritte's carte blanch forest,
moving ever towards

its native cypress, cedar, almond
– that final ace pulled
from its spotted sleeve –
even an artist couldn't hold it for long.

The first time I ever saw
the ocelot, it was labelled
*leopardus pardalis;*
a twiggish ribcage
and the rest displayed
behind glass
in an undead menagerie.
Its humerus, I thought,
you could almost use to eat
Chow Mein,
or pin up your hair.

Now, I hear,
they're together again,
in Paris, I guess, Barcelona,
or New York,
they're hanging out once more,
best mates; this time, no doubt,
the ocelot is sure
to keep his pet on shorter leash;
his 'tache well-waxed,
swigging absinthe,
knocking it back,
smug eye sockets unswivelling
in surveillance of the room,
all these friendly corpses
they both recall,
all now gathered here in this
*memento mori* landscape.

*Katie Allen*

# OLD DOGS

'They're shutting down the circus,' they announced,
and when the snows swept north, the buyers came,
hands digging in wallets. The sultans pounced;
the cheetahs were swiftly auctioned off, same
with the trick ponies; fought over by dads
for daughters velveted in riding hats.
The scraggy elephants - the troupe were glad
to shrug off; they turned them loose. The big cats
they killed for fur. The lion tamer cried.
The clowns raised pints to hide their lolling smiles.
Years on, an ex-acrobat wept beside
her lover's bones; hiccupped out denial,
tore blossoms from her hair. There's nothing gained
in draining all the heavens. Rain is rain.

*Katie Allen*

## SCOPE SONNENIZIO

Let those who are in favour with their stars*
scan all those horoscopes left lying in rooms
designed for waiting. My stars and I – we rarely see
quite eye-to-eye. But if you're one of those described,
don't let me put you off. Instead let those
you've never met tell you just who you are.
They know your star sign, and so they know
the perfume you should wear, your favoured
flirting style. Do me a favour: ask yourself this –
did those writers, did they brandish telescopes
at night, tottering in their stilettos, just to tell
those Aquarians - newsflash! – don't wear red
this week? The stars you see are old; of the past,
not future. Let this month's horoscope be your last.

*Katie Allen*

*Opening line from Shakespeare's *Sonnet 25*.

# DARK-HAIRED BOY

Sat there, dark hair can't compare to the way you stare
at the orb in your palm, so calm with the whole universe

there in your hand, lighting up your face, out of place
in the dark air. You hold the stars, you

hold the globe. Why, you might even hold Shakespeare
I suppose. Great mystery, never ending, yet is it you

or the light that is bending? Sending hope to the open
circle who ever employ you, as the beacon light, so steely,

so distant, so right, with your wire hair—there, I wrote it,
paid homage to that coral sonnet. Now, back to the stars,

back to the universe, back to the pocket of my purse, where
I hold the subject of all of your desires; whilst you hold the stars.

*Vicki Benson*

# HEATHROW MEOW

We invert port of call to get
call of port, so that

ports can summon vocally. Some
bleat, some bark, but dumb

as it sounds — hark! Now
it comes: the Heathrow meow.

We get Heathrow meow
from he threw me out

(just before tea)
and when he does it comes to me:

*meow*. How unlike a cat
an airport is. In the cab

to Terminal 3 the air is clear of flying fur
and free of fear I hear the purr.

*Peter Blegvad*

[Figure A]
Here are two gentlemen & a lady
contemplating a length of dug-up pipeline.


[Fig. B]
Figure B. illustrates the assertion:
"ambiguity can't be measured
like a change in temperature."


[Fig. C]
Figure C. consists of
a list of
assorted equipage,
a gentleman imagines
how the items on the list would look
if only part exhumed.
He thinks they wouldn't look
unlike a length of pipe.

Or a rung.
(When you remove a rung from a ladder
the whole is suddenly part, the part is whole.
But the hue & temperature
of a pipeline
are ineluctably parts, without the pipeline
they would cease to be.)

[Fig. D]
Anything you care to mention
of 3 dimensions
like a length of pipe,
in a certain light
can be seen as the projection or the shadow of
an entity of 4 dimensions.
See Figure D.

*Peter Blegvad*

# FOR A HORSE

Everyone's talking about childhood, how it was,
how it ought to be, how it's under siege, how to
return to it. In Fourier's utopian *Phalanstère*
a 10 year old was king.

My own kingdom, the realm of myself, is no utopia.
It's mob rule. Sometimes an old crone is on the throne
issuing severe edicts. Sometimes she's middle aged and
*laissez faire*. Sometimes she's my mother. Other times

a bald tot smears excrement on the frescoes and
no one stops him because he's more than a king,
the tot is god. God or not, he needs a good slap.
Where's his father? He's not an orphan, exactly,

but he is his own father and mother. He doesn't
know what he wants so he can't be satisfied.
Luckily his reign is periodic and soon my sister,
my twin, has my kingdom safely

in hand. Sensible girl. Prudent.
She cups her hand around the candle
of my kingdom to protect its flickering
flame. She guides it out into the garden

to illuminate a few things. She shows us
the night blooming lily. She lifts her skirts
to illuminate her own vulva.
The correspondence is remarkable.

The populace adore her, but
next morning Trotsky's in charge
imposing a new order.
The order is for sandwiches, *sandwiches*

*for all!* When the aristocracy is restored,
Lord Sandwich rules a while, but then, at
last, it's bedtime. I exhale my kingdom in a
sigh of happy abdication. As I sleep

it floats above me, a ribbon of astral
tissue, a little paler than the dark,
as if lit by a wristwatch, or
by a few lost flakes of scurf,
*les neiges dantan.*

*Peter Blegvad*

# GLYPH

*In all of the pre-Columbian New World, only the Maya can be said to have
possessed true writing, if we define that as human speech made visible.*

At first the Bishop asked her for the truth,
that blandly Latin script that ploughed his tongue,
but each new symbol, sound to fit the glyphs
would contradict his righteous alphabet
and so he found a clue in singeing flesh:
her drowning, hanging footless from the pine.

And yet her words would fly to him as birds,
years later when the speaker was long dead:
often the hummingbird's red-throated whir;
the vulture's prod for jelly, beak for eyes;
stern eagles swooping on his Indian fig,
while nets retrieved the mystery of cranes.

How could he know tenors of stony glyphs,
their mathematics of an ageing sky.
He sensed a toothless woman in the moon,
but missed the honey harvest of the fly.
He never saw a crone shoulder the sun,
nor knew the lighthouse of the northern star.

The tally of misreading soon advanced
so legions of proud glyphs were rapt by flames,
but speaking in the ballast-base of clay,
new villages were made from wet leaf-beds,
where souls escape to buzz about the pines
and ripening flowers are budding to be read.

*Zoë Brigley*

# THE TIN SOLDIER

On the night of her marriage, she presses
her cold forehead against her bridegroom's cheek
as they look through the window over golden city spires
that glow under sunset like the dream of a promise.

Looking into the fall of darkness is like gazing
into a shroud: a woman veiled white like a bride
and black in the Spanish lace of a mourner,
with a face underneath of plaster and porcelain.

Lately she finds that her head will not fit the pillow
when she lies in bed at her bridegroom's side,
because the room is small and flickers by candlelight
and the air is thick with the taste of molten metal.

She still remembers the stories of her childhood
and if she is the ballerina, fashioned in paper,
self-consuming by flame, then he must be the tin soldier,
fighting flood, fear, appetite to carry home his white-hot heart.

*Zoë Brigley*

## THE BLUE ROSE
### i.m. James Ernest Brigley

His roses grew in my grandmother's flowerbeds,
in the garden where the pale green gate fitted the latch
awkwardly. The word, *rose*, as well travelled as he was:
*rosa* the Latin made from the Greek *rhodea*
from Aramaic *wurdda* that mimics Iranian *warda*.
Late in his garden, blooms that bowed to his stoop
now pay him remembrance; the fine Floribunda
Miniature Cupcake and hardy Polyantha.

Not Nyasaland figs or the Belizian black orchid, but
the Queen Elizabeth, Comanche and Montezuma.
The Great Maiden's Blush, the Song of the Stars
and Tangerine Jewel give way to his tools.
The Impressionist, Teasing Georgia, Chianti, Othello,
Petit de Hollande, Climbing Peace and American Pillars
squint in their fury. The Alba rose wet in the dew,
Gallica, Damask, Tamora: all pay their dues.

The twiggy Green Rose, Crimson China and Crested Sweet Heart
are as staunch in their thanks as the Stanwell Perpetual,
while Dainty Bess, Gray Pearl and reddening Vesuvius
shrink in grief to a Penny Ante or tiny Tom Thumb.
In the late silence of his rooms without gardens,
did he lift the latch on the pale green gate to find
a riot of thorns, a wilderness of bourbons, as sweet
and pungent as a dose of dopamine to the brain?

Or only the ripening blue rose of forgetfulness
tended by his care, growing beyond remembering
as full as a moon and still in bloom.

*Zoë Brigley*

# MY PEAR TREE BOWER

*The nun's pear tree stood up a tall dryad skeleton, grey, gaunt and stripped.*
*A thought struck me - one of those queer fantastic thoughts that will sometimes*
*strike solitary people. I put on my bonnet, cloak and furs, and went out into the city.*
　　　　Charlotte Brontë

On a quest to find you, after journeys by sea,
sickened by waves and cursed by sailors,
I find myself a nun in a silent oratory
wishing for speech in a low and gloomy room
lit by a crucifix and the vigil of two candles.

A child, I sleep in my narrow bed, as the stove
spits chips and fills the room with smoke.
Beyond my lattice grill is the thud of branches
on the window: a broken pear tree
calls me to haunt the startled orchard.

The purple anthers of pear tree blossom,
stiffen with fright; flowers fall away to snow
revealing the brown-rot of blackened branches.
One pear tree above others is my own Methuselah
—a granite slab at its roots hides a crypt.

Deep and leafy in my seclusion,
I wait for the fruiting of my giant pear tree,
the honey of its pendulous fruit.
Now for the stripping of my narrow skirt:
the becoming skeleton of the nunning pear tree.

Unwind my bandage, my chalked veil,
as the tongue finds carpel, seed and pip,
and at the heart of the pear, your eye
reveals itself to have known of my coming,
to have watched me all along.

*Zoë Brigley*

# THE CRESCENT OF HEARING

## 1587

You hear tides. Where the tale outwears the teller
is a wide turn, slow at the tiller.
Good news travels slower,

not a rainbow portrait, not all ears.
Each new gust of the swelling cheek
blows scattered rumour,

leaves the listener drydocked: the Duke of Parma's
troops idling in Dunkirk, Medina Sedona's
crescent of ships at anchor.

Fear's a great converser. Pass it on,
tongue-heavy, pendant, thin as bell's bronze
gone chap-worn, after a year of terrors.

Or later, wonders, jetsam with such details
as neeptide doubloons shingling Donegal.

## 1637

*The Archbishop of Canterbury, being informed by his spies*
*what Mr Prynne said, moved the Lords then sitting*
*in the Star Chamber that he might be gagged*
*and have some further censure to be presently*
*executed on him; but that motion did not succeed.*
*Mr Burton spake much while in the pillory to the people.*
*The executioner cut off his ears deep and close,*
*in a cruel manner, with much effusion of blood,*
*an artery being cut, as there was likewise of Dr Bastwick.*
*Then Mr Prynne's cheeks were seared with an iron*
*made exceeding hot; which done, the executioner*
*cut off one of his ears and a piece of his cheek*

*with it; then hacking the other ear almost off,*
*he left it hanging and went down; but being called*
*up again he cut it quite off.*


## 1737

A shrivelled *casus belli* in the Commons,
the boxed once-ear of Captain Jenkins
is seven years of cartilage and pickle.
Like snuff or contraband, like a bad joke
this dumb witness passes round the Frontbench.
The Speaker puts the question, the tellers count.


## 1937

Tintin searches for the broken eared fetish,
ends up in San Theodoros as a colonel
[3487 colonels
but only 49 corporals in that army].
Promise of quarantine
        for aggressor nations,
a bullet
for the last Balinese tiger.
Toscanini's                    Christmas;
        peaceful radio

Ivor Gurney dies, speaking to Schubert.

*James Brookes*

# MONS HORSE BURIAL

Haunch of a 13-pounder, mud-locked. One pelvic wheel.
The barrel down-tilt, something of a horse
straddling it. At half dismount
the trooper, dirigible angel, splays his flanks.

Gingerly he's unhooked from his embrace
and the left stirrup. The gun-horse —
mane down over its confusion
of muzzles — maintains dressage balance

and poses the usual problem for the Detail.
Steak-stripped since the shell burst,
the last consummation's been had of it.
There's no petrol, a wood fire won't take.

Even clay, after some debate, and much
struggle toward the ditch, rejects its frame.
A week of repeat salvos — the parapet's
weak soil flensed to an equine shrapnel.

*James Brookes*

# CONCERNING PLUNDER

On your coccyx, a gold contusion
holds the sinews, rope-braid tarred
to the treasure-ship of
your listing body.

I hurry to kiss it,
with the old piracy
woven into us
before torques were ravelled.

My not-ancestors, the White Rajahs
gave Sarawak a gold-fielded ensign;
but it never turned
to an honest Gibraltar.

I plant my kisses
on your spine's base,
to the crack of your
*terra nullius.*

I've seen the blueprint of the slave ship *Brookes,*
the melded cargo of its wooden gut
is at least in part
my inheritance.

And this house that holds
seven tenths of my life
will never keep you,
though the hold stays tight

as my roving dog
and the stick in his mouth
loosed on the fields
forgives my horror

that the branch in his maw
like a spar or a mast
is the still fur-clad
foreleg of a deer,

a leg that once sailed
in a whole perfect craft
never threatening to spill
its slight ingots of bone.

*James Brookes*

# REQUIEM FOR AN INVASION

*The dice of drowned men's bones he saw bequeath*
*An embassy*
      Hart Crane

By freight going landward,
half of the *Mary Rose*
sleeping through polyphonies of weather.

A hand snagged in the water.
Trowels and airlifts and gently wafting silt.
Whorled, our native churchyard verdigris,
across the steeps
of chalk-familiar cloud, the hills of samphire.

Up, up we went, through the cleft of marriage,
as though it needed to take
only our arm past the elbow, to heft and salvage.

When did the clutch-bone current find us out?
Loved enemy, let
our ribs slant and meet
as fingers at prayer
our hearts a tumbled brace of Whitby jet.

*James Brookes*

# DAWN IN DORSET

You will find it in the bee-scream of a tent zip
and the rush of air through the fly-sheet
then the rustle of shoes on plastic
as you try not to step on a peg.

Fasten the door and leave her
to fill the dome with her dreams
while you walk off the trappedness
of a roof two feet from your face.

Let the green creep up to your ankles
as you crawl to the car, climb
into the boot and cry at last.
Nobody is here to hurt you.

Coiled foetal over the spare tyre
you can think anything.

*Phil Brown*

# SIR GAWAIN ON THE NORTHERN LINE

*'In god fayth,' quoth the goode knight, 'Gawan I hatte,*
*That bede the this buffet, quat-so bifalles after,*
*And at this tyme twelmonyth take at the another*
*Wyth what weppen so thou wylt, and with no wyy elles*
       *on lyve.'*

and if fate should fling me onto
the electric rail of a tube's tracks
to be sliced open with steel wheels
let me stay so mangled as to remain
unidentifiable and let the driver lose
       no sleep.

Or if my end should be the slow sort
made more moral
with each cigarette I suck to the tip
allow me the time to close my accounts
and make good on old
       promises.

Let death deal me the bravery to apologise
for piquant truths and pretty lies
and let my last words yield
more answers than questions
and the humility to acquiesce to
       all suggestions.

Let my obituary eat up no more column
inches than those not born into old money
and should I be murdered at alighting
in Burnt Oak amid the fourth concentric
Zone let the artist of my death
       escape.

The terms, though not of my choice, were agreed
and as I course viral underneath this metropolis
I leave my regrets at Embankment, Euston, Camden Town
like a skin shed, baring my raw jelly.
No more words sir, my naked neck is
      rightly yours.
   The night deliquesces us all
   under the looming street-lamp necks
   to be human altrical
   in the city's warp and weft.

*Phil Brown*

# TABA

Cut from the side of a mountain
in a world where the wind's a warm breath,

the transplant town under Israel's eyebrow
imports its own country's culture.

A pentagram of hotels photoshopped into the desert
like abaci hung in a jungle.

At sun-up the horizon's a grey forever
but Jordan's lights line the night's horizon.

I never think of you, Kathryn,
but the buffet included a cauldron of humus

and an inexhaustible pile of warm pitas,
I expect just reading those words makes you happy.

Friday's a faux-festival in the town
they parade a camel outside the sham shisha-bar

and a child does a short dance of sorts
before returning to his bracelet stall.

I got sun-stroke on the first day of Ramadan,
sweated it out under the hum of the air-con

eventually leaving into the warm roar of the evening
perspiring in the breeze I broke fast.

Mumbling *shokran* at the waiter
as I pass him his tip in American dollars I realise

nothing. My hands are cut from coral, my arms
are unliftable and I realise nothing.

*Phil Brown*

# PAWS: AN OBSESSION

I look at you, rolling dogs,
with envy.

You get away with so much,
having paws.

You've eaten my chair but it's okay
because you offer me your paw
and I'm gone.

Imagine if I, too, could have them!
The snoring commuter lolling next to me
on the train, slapped across the cheek
with an innocent paw. He'd laugh and nod
the other way.

Serious cats on the fence,
I salute you. Your paws give way
to claws which grip and tear and rip
(if necessary).

You get away with so much,
having paws.

*Claire Bunyan*

# FAILED DOVE RELEASE

You'd expect them to fly,
I guess –
not squat coiled up
like rusted feathered springs,
unaware.

Where are the dark-eyed
white-winged paper airplanes,
screaming to freedom?

Perhaps we are the children
who folded incorrectly,
the unstreamlined, uneducated, unloved –

weeping now, staring out blind
at a box of empty doves.

*Claire Bunyan*

# TO A PIPISTRELLE

Forgive us our early evening summer drinks,
our interference to your fine-tuned reception,
our wittering across unoaked Chardonnay,
Stan Getz or Arvo Pärt drifting your way
with the nicknames you won't get (Big Dee,
Hodge-Podge) past sonics and a titter
of accompanying laughter that maybe
draws you down come dusk: full tilt Billy
Whizz, gut-curving bullet dive, liquorice sheen,
an even giggle and then back on up to an Arts
and Crafts chimney, registering an exit to light.

*Peter Carpenter*

## FALSE OAT GRASS – A FIGURE OF EIGHT WALK
### for Amanda

Crawling boards circa nineteen forty five,
Dutch ladders, lethality and vulnerability
Testing equipment for Blenheims, concrete
Posts, lichen-scored, collapsed timberwork
Among teasels, miked up, like sea holly,
Choco-rust, re-inforced poppy bunker blocks,
Coins, nerve-centres for ballistics, timing
Beacons, copper thieves, control freak desks –
Basically they bombed the shit out of it,
Shingle and military kit, and lo on a level
The long glory of tankers watch-strapped
To the sea-line, jellyfish pagoda, abrupt
Shingle plunge, swales, contorted riveting,
Native speakers, all on the website, I expect:

All on the website, riveting native speakers,
Contorted swales, abrupt shingle plunge,
Jellyfish pagoda, I expect, watch-strapped
To the sea-line, the long glory of tankers
And lo on a level, shingle and military kit,
(Basically they bombed the shit out of it );
Control freak desks, copper thieves, timing
Beacons, nerve-centres for ballistics, coins,
Re-inforced poppy bunker blocks, choco-
Rust, collapsed timberwork in teasels, like
Sea holly, miked up, concrete posts lichen-
Scored, lethality and vulnerability testing
Equipment for Blenheims, Dutch ladders,
Crawling boards circa nineteen forty five.

*Peter Carpenter*

# LAWNMOWERER

Hey Dad, what else do you call someone who uses a lawnmower?
When your friends come ask who I am, it isn't funny
when you say that I am just the free-loading gardener
who can't do anything except cut the grass inadequately.
It also isn't funny when you say, "Well done, son,"
with the irony effervescent in its brutally crushing flow
because my lifetime achievements fit inside a crouton,
and I know.

Hey Dad, when I was asleep on the sofa when you came home
from work, and you called me a lazy slacker, did you know
that my eyes weren't closed?

        I was just watching something
invisible.
I was watching the photo on the mantelpiece of the three of us: your hair
cut like lemons, and Mum still wearing that perfume she left behind.

Hey Dad, I wish you would remember when I was twelve,
and I played the thief in the school play and stole the show.
You were so proud you let me sit in the front seat of the car,
but now I have to use a sleeping bag on the basement floor
instead of the sofa where we used to sit watching football together,
drinking beer, making small talk about your job and the weather.

Hey Dad, shall I tell you what I remember?
I remember when I was three, and you told me dragons didn't exist.
I remember you telling me I was an accident
in front of your friends,

       in front of my first girlfriend,

           in front
of the teachers at parents' evening
(the only one which you actually went to).
I remember being thirteen and writing the script for a zombie film
told from the zombies' perspective. I called it "Night of the Sparkling
Apple Jazz".
You called it a waste of time, son.

You said my potential is like The Smiths reforming – it's never going to happen, son.

Hey Dad, I'm not going to apologise for ruining your jumper by turning it
into a peninsula; cutting the sleeves made me feel like I was a marathon runner
ripping the finishing line. And I'm definitely not going to apologise on your behalf,
because she's left and never coming back, because that's what happens when you spend
a lifetime trying to make being selfish an endearing characteristic, so we might as well cancel
the newspaper subscription, but if you do this week's crossword, the final word is
L-A-W-N-M-O-W-E-R-E-R; it is a real word, so if you're going to insult me
every day, at least use the right terminology, even though it is arguably not true
 like how I still call you Dad. I'm sorry, Dad.

*Nick Chen*

# SOMETHING

Whatever it was, it began as a fly in the room,
came in through the window and stuttered about
on our pillows and shoulders with shit on its feet,
hummed while we slept, and made itself at home.

We noticed it once it had swelled to the size of a cat:
curled up at the edge of the mattress and quietly taking
up more than its actual size, or, when we tried making
love, looking up, affronted. No coaxing would shift it –

it seemed to lose shape but  hold fast, bloated and slack,
a life of its own between us. It stuck in our minds
like the girl in that story our friends told us once in the pub:

she loved her snake, and thought it loved her back,
let it stretch in her bed like a tape-measure, only to find
it was waiting to grow to full size, when it swallowed her up.

*Swithun Cooper*

# THE LASTING DEAD

*The Hunterian Museum, Royal College of Surgeons*

The men in here have skin that peels away
from the root of the face, like a climbing harelip,
muscles strung out into strips of wound,
fat pumped with pigment. Some rest in their bells,
soaked in formaldehyde, whitened by acid
to something more like marble. Some are dry

and hang among the open guts of girls
who died whilst giving birth, their abdomens
side by side with a shining chunk of skull
belonging to a four year old. Her skin
and eyelashes and hair intact, she seems
to be asleep, dreaming of the rest of her.

The skeleton of flesh that firmed to bone
and fused its owner shut like a rusted door
has stayed together through the century:
through blasts of war, when the building's front
was blown away as neatly as the face
of the soldier sketched along the upstairs wall.

To have come across the rubble of these rooms,
have reached beneath, found slices of corpse
and, recognising each, rebuilt the place
out of the lasting dead. To be their surgeon,
to blindly lift the skin, feel threads beneath,
and still to know exactly where you are.

*Swithun Cooper*

# MIRROR/DRYCH

The accidental sun can be seen through          the mirror
the scar in the sky as I skate out,          is smeared with
(ysglefrio mas i'r canol o'r llyn)          my fingerprints
over underbelly greens & jaded blues.          & with a cuff
A lash slides into my eye as I slide          I polish it clean.
into the lake. I tend to line the mirror          the lake
with the curve of my lid. (rwy'n edrych          is perfect,
yn y drych yn y gaeaf)          under winter skies untouched.

The snow falls in avalanchine proportions          suddenly,
(mae'n bwrw eira!) covering          from nowhere,
the blues & greens & aquamarines,          lucky salt spills,
covering my skates it's blown all over,          fine as flour

& the scar in the sky widens          tapped from a sieve,
& the sun reflects pathetically off the lake          so clean
& my own reflection is pathetic also,          it squeaks
I watch how my red nose runs.          when you squeeze it.

The snow settles soon enough,          now I score through,
a downy sheet of white.          slicing parallel pathways.

It is clearly          it's being made up into perfect lines
the most beautiful of all seasons.          (llinellau o gwyn)

I cut through the snow,          as I splice each droplet.
skating in lines          then I line the mirror with the curve

(rwy'n torri trwy'r eira fel cyllell)          of my lid
until the mirror's gleaming.          Before the wind blows.

*Nicola Davidson*

# THE BADGER STONE

n met a fayrie of the lore
who told me of her mother moor

with lines in whispers half begun
n tricks the bits of what she sung

that u should take-the sheepy paths
-she doesn't like the 1's the people put

-she'll get u lost-she'll move her stones-
so u should always go barefoot

sing barefoot across the moor
don't steal her berries-they're not urs

2 quiet fayrie n incomplete-
-n stain your wicked hands and feet

she'll move her paths-my mother queen
-more n more-n never b seen

*David Devanny*

# THE HANGING STONE

sing wind
sing bracken sheaves
sing Saxons go away

replace their tools
with bog-bean spools
n cottongrass cambric grey

dress the wet peat land
as grassy mounds
with asphodel and milkwort hey

sing wind
sing whortleberry leaf
sing Saxons go away

ask the mountain ferns
2 curl the rocks
so none of their walls will stay

n while they're sleeping
make them itch – stick
round–leaved–sundew where they lay

sing wind
sing fertile moray grains
sing Saxons go away

*David Devanny*

# THE BARMISHAW STONE

*an answer 2 'me father bought me an acre o land'*
look out 4 that chick with the
psychedelic hand-knitted beanie
often seen clinging 2
Finnay yellowed paperback the Whitby witches

n if u do run in2 her
give her my best
n in ur fittest voice
tell her yes

- tell her yes
if she'll knit me
a thigh high dress
if she'll crotchet a jaguar
then maybe – i guess

-tell her yes
if she knits herself
some sexy lingerie
if she weaves herself some self-esteem
that witch may get a lay

tell her yes

tell her yes

if she always looks her best

if she sews a gorgeous private jet
n smokes those knitted cigarettes
then yes – of course – its yes

*David Devanny*

# DISCOMEDUSAE

It felt like newborn silk;
the wrapping on them. It
puckered its lips like a sneering
flower, It was almost made of feathers.
They were a horde of plumed whales finding
somewhere to die; they shuddered and swelled;
lungs unused to oxygen. Toxic patterning, a nuclear
explosion when it went through her feet, having wriggled
out of its swaddling. It had grown more fingers than it realised
and used them like antennae, octopussing its way across my face
In lashing ripples. We saw them off the hulls in volcanic rims,
pulsating with transparent luminescence like organic gloves;
cloudy monocles for tuna fish. There is room for Bourgeois
in the oceans. I'd hoped the dilated mouth would close
but it gaped still, pouring frills and feelers like saliva.
We wandered how they'd fornicate—because they
could not make love without a backbone.
I processed their flexing scalps for a
helmet with a noxious lining.
the curtain of needle hairs
fell through me, and
I spent time learning
from them how
to breathe
through
my palms.

*Rebecca Fearnley*

# MAN IN THE METEORITE

I

We found him in a net
of spider webs bleeding
battery fluid, counted the pixels
in his eyes; proclaimed a diagnosis
of madness. He was a wounded
machine. We called him Earl.

In the shadows of his eyes
as our hands caught at his wires
we taught him what it meant to cry.
He practised by himself, trying
variations of volume from the cupboard
in which we had locked him.

We tried to train him to walk—
for the purpose of later teaching him
to fall-but he had wheels and could only roll.
He crawled like a broken locomotive
around the parts of past
he remembered to find and

stopped to blink at our faces
while we unscrewed his arms
and used them as swords. He recorded
our faces and the baring of teeth,
made his own word for our laughing.

II

We took him to a narrow beach,
let him sink in the sand while we
built a snow-queen from mulch,
from rogue-snowflakes. In the evening
we spied him beside her with his fingers
outstretched to ask for her hand.

At dawn he crushed a purple
flower, showered it over himself
and his sand-girl. They tried
to find a way to kiss but one
of us was a puritan, and we
kicked our queen back to dust.


We poured salt-water down
his throat to see if it would make
him sick, took turns peering past
his tongue to watch the inside rust.
We wondered what happened
to metal when it reached puberty.

Earl's voice didn't break and we broke
it for him, made him our spokesman
when we'd done something wrong.

It was here, in this hole in the earth
where the meteor hit that we
kick-started his heart and fed

his silicon soul to the dark.

*Rebecca Fearnley*

# THE BIPOLAR BEAR

Stiff tundra air can make her sleeping patterns bitty,
She knows this and attempts to communicate such
But the knowledge of post-natal depression
Has not yet come to the ice floes
Or the backs of bear's minds when they maul
And beg her for food.
Sunlight is scarce,
She finds herself relying more heavily
On her serotonin level than is regularly observed
In specimens of her size.
Perhaps akin to some form of diabetes,
Whatever gland allows her to regulate her endorphins
Is defunct.
And how is she to know there are two ice caps
And that the dizziness is due to a tilted axis?

Ursidae is a weighty language
And translation takes some time before
He is able to fully understand
The seriousness of her mental glaciation.
His diagnosis is swift
And somewhat lacking;

'she has discarded all phenotypes
And resorted to a behaviour one can only describe as
Baffling.'

Owls make terrible therapists.

*Rebecca Fearnley*

# THE DRIVE

Drizzle fills up every parking space
in a systematic *coup d'état* of the street.
I'm still irritated by yesterday's forecast
so I crash the car into the rain
to let you know just how much I hate
this.

This:
a damp journey through the traffic of shared space
where wardens direct the raging street
down and out, up and out, up down and cast
out onto the curb, into the rain:
this thing I hate.

I hate
this:
the space
the street
and all its cast
of rain.

You comment on the rain:
'This weather's awful,' you say, 'I hate
this country.' (That's all; just this.)
You cannot understand the space
– outside of us is beyond you – 'it's just a street
for God's sake, a street where I happen to—' and we're cast.

We're so suitably cast
together in this cluttering rain.
You know you say 'hate' with such hate
(you know how to say words like this
with such feeling.) You give them space
to breed. My car is parked in your street,

lost in the lights of a widening street
gorged to the brim and cast
in a glaze of rain.
You want to hate
all of this
but you dare not find the space.

Our space
is cast.
I hate this rain.

*Chloe Todd Fordham*

Oak turning silver birch when she touched,
    or was it just the silent spill of white
developing the copse in stills of blanched
hoarfrost? Cyan, yellow, magenta, light –
then the stop of the shutter click shut
settling her finger forever against the bark.

She was the subject for some sort of a Paradise,
    peeking out like a Pre-Raphaelite
miniature, her smile widening life
towards the instant of mine, just not quite.
(As if she knew how many hours were left
until we'd crawl into the next underworld.)

I'm losing my hair to the balding boughs.
    The silver-grey of temples
steals away and a black crow
stalks the day in tufts of grey to grapple
the fall of night. *Not yet*, she smiled.
She beamed, *just be*. Hand me down, to the best fits

of infancy. Catch me, in the eye of 16mm.
    Watch the wing-span of her palm
collect the landscape of my face, trace
the pelt of my brow and tickle the stem.
At three months, she felt the earth crust over
the veins beneath the bark of every branching limb.

At three months, she knew the snap of a broken
    lens, and the cool quiet of darkened rooms.
She's crawling the root, hands down;
fingering the light-tight box;
touching the torso of ashen skin:
my blood oaked in silver birch.

*Chloe Todd Fordham*

# VERTICAL

Screaming I lift her onto the table:
three hands make up her body until they snag
snug under her tiny arms. I don't know
who is holding harder, who is wanting harder
to be held by the sheer incline of
him: the big log bears her tongue-tied tip-toe
forward on the flat. *Pit-pat, pit-pat, pat.*
All around, the kitchen clutched in *hush.*
*There there!* her hand-made paws crawl
over his chest: the days when they could touch.
Hush is all around then – and scream: a rare *purr*
cracking the tiles stiffly as a body stalks
the negative space of vertical. Spine up, hind
leg down and waiting for her toe to tip
over the edge of the oil-daubed oak-field,
shaved down cheek and splintered chin
        (nudging me to let go for him).
She is standing for the very first time
twelve baby-feet above and anchored by ankle-
roots, strong trunks of calf then thigh: table legs.
She is standing now, in still-life on dead-oak,
wondering at how upright the world is, how
Taut.
I go to pick up the screaming phone, let go
of her stare for the first time to make the noise
stop, go. *Pit-pat. Ring-ring. Hush.* The crash
of a screaming sapling falling, spine-down;
the split of the hind-leg as it hits a horizontal
        unhinged, jangling world.

And I'm holding her toes like tiny hands,
clutching her awkward scream, asking her if she's ok.

*Chloe Todd Fordham*

# CULTURE ANTI-HERO

*The Heist*

Top soil churns and drifts of sand plume,
around a fire four men sat in costume,
smudging the arid air with smoke-
on dust, permeating distrust;

a scent of rebellion or off-milk in heat.

Huddled in tribe thumbing through blue prints,
to the river bank where language is held
under lock and key.

Each man wore a mask of a beast at ease,
crude constructions of fur with two eye holes.
A look serene, jumping with fleas
and all the more ominous lit by the hot coals.

The sun cowered to the darkened eyelid of night
and the campfire grew bright in defiance.
The men sang like fire-water kites,
side winding to their own beat.

Until at long last,
no longer able to defer their sleep,
a final sigh from each.
A nod to tomorrow, the just out of reach,
tucked behind the arithmetic of sheep.

First to fall
a man complied of water and mist,
elusive in flesh,
masked as a broad-faced Potoroo.

The next to quiver to the nightman's song
a man of all wrong geometry.
An Atlas Bear who punched cows in the wrong
and pungent to the lowest degree.

Followed swiftly by the slumber gripped third,
a Bali Tiger of neat oil slick croon.
A pretty boy and crack shot inferred
to whom the round-heeled ladies swooned.

The last still long danced the fire pit,
shouldering a sea.
He cast shadow animals on rocks at each ebb.
He was 'The Curley Wolf of Dread Black Matted Locks'.

A blowhard beast and leader of the pack.
He was a rhinestone shepherd, a real hero,
always ahead three swigs of who-hit-jack
with a nerve as cool as glacier ice.

Daybreak shatters with a birdsong of glass
illuminating in detail all things blue.
Sharp edged the hairy finger grass swayed,
caked in the dust of long dead dew.

The horses stirred, three studs and a filly,
appaloosa, sorrel, roan and white,
hoofs to the sagebrush ready for flight.
So the gang set off at an easy three-bit gait,
four long shadows of morning men riding.

The road was paved with shoals
where the water seemed to defy its level
to slide over the rocks.

To each side, vast structures of adamant
piled unlike mountains.
All of a sandy stone with a splash of lime.
Mottles, dark patches,
flicked on like molten iron.

A sound-scene of storm gods,
strumming at stalactites
in a harmony of claw and tentacle.

Then kingfisher.
Electric blue. Best-seen best effect
when 'bird' observed in low-level flight
speeding over streaming topaz
shadow-chased by emeralds.
The deeper fishes shrug.
Characteristic
of sublime marine life.

Pack to the posse,
the destination grew close,
approaching them as a tower.

It the crowning glory of the delta;
a single bank built up
as if an invisible wall required scaling.
In the old days the door was guarded.
Now two cosmic bone piles
decorate the porch in symmetry.

A tender quake of dismount-feet landing
resonated and was the signal to begin;
blood metals galvanised.

A note aside, concealed
in the chamber of each gun
a sum sufficient for burial.

The Curley Wolf raises his snout to smell
the debris of fate that lingers air bound;
the end zone of all gunslingers
who keep true to a dire causality
but become the subject of folk singers and history.

Frog-leg fingers twitch, trigger-happy
but disappointed, subsequently,
at the single clerk within.

The wizened Clerk sighed, his nametag lost.
His shoulders were padded with sediment,
two white-collar bones in need of a brush.
His beard a chain, tethered to a ball
of its own mass twiddled by thumbs,
or coughed up by some celestial cat.

The wolf hero, bulk, pretty boy and brains
wore intention clear in their faces,
so the clerk gestured them down,
through a stairwell and a gullet.
In the belly of the bank the water was black
and it felt like a fishbowl.

The safe sat centred,
spot lit by imported light.
Nested upon it a swan.

Strolling with ancient protocol in his step
the clerk approached alone.
He drew a pipe and instead of playing,
passed it to the swan in peace.
The swan flew off;
the pipe being what the bird was waiting on.

From his top pocket the clerk now drew a box.
Opened it and out flew a small gadfly
that B-lined to its work on the locks
and with its job complete it said 'Goodbye'.

The safe door creaked if you listen so clear
opening a void no bigger than a thumb.
It was large to begin, but shrank as it grew wider.
By the time the door was fully a jar
you could barely fit a pickle in.
All leaned in to see what they could hear
but no sound travelled and they still stood dumb.

The Atlas Bear tilted a head askew
and the Bali Tiger leant on the wall.
all casual-like for lack of a pew.
The Curley Wolf approached,
bent down on one knee,
reached out a single index finger
and entered as you would a cup of tea,
- slowly- and inside a moment linger.

The retraction was quick, raised to the nose
paused, for the mask to be lifted, and in.
The object of their desire,
the bounty and the boon.

It was lost in The Great Strain Days,
'The Smell of Rain',
put in a box and stowed away.

Not being a prize of two parts
it was time to get a way.
Outside the sun hit them in splinters
and each blinked twice.

The delta was flooded with Last Words,
an army marching to the sound
of a silent alarm.

The clerk removed his beard
and stepped over the line;
the gang statues.

Four notes and masks were retrieved.

'The Curley Wolf of Dread Black Matted Locks'
shot, but not dead.
Found on the floor smiling
with his finger up his nose.

The Last Words cut it off
put it back in the box,
it still resides there now,
safe and sound.

And they tethered him up, way out in Caucasus,
hammered Megara into the ground
to prevent any tampering.
Charged him with armed robbery
and attempted arson.
It broke him,
and then he ended up on the rocks,
with fingers scotch.
He tried to drink himself to death
but his liver held up.

*James Harringman*

# CORMORANT

You scan the bay and always see one—
perched like a discarded coat on some
purposeful post of sea-bleached wood.

Oil-black, slick—yet slightly scragged
around the neck, set down without care
and ready, because there is no space

no then-now or here-there
except that which can be flown through
or dived into with a half-jump

to go deeper, to precisely grasp fish,
water snakes, small eels. If you could see that,
if you could see them underwater,

being a different shape,
then this world would not be as it is.
They cry out to the city leaveleave

or nothingisasitseems. Offcuts of night—
for the night is made of them,
is when they come in  squalls to the coast

and rest outside your window.
Your hair dried wiry with salt air
you pretend not to notice them,

watch tv. They're there again in the morning
appearing as hastily hung hats.
You see them extend their necks, preen themselves

or they stand spread-winged for a second
blazon onto your eye like a motto
—you point one out to me,

say, Ilovethecormorants, they are alwaysthere.

*Emily Hasler*

# NATURAL HISTORY

*Where the men of science wear their eternity*
*with the attitude of clergymen or giants.*

Here in the least-lit corner of the museum
your skin is an affectation. Your hair dulls
and your eyesockets deepen. You collect
shadow, the clatter of feet, polished rock,

ironwork, stuttered light through tiny panes.
See the joins. Latin erected into names,
stumbles into steps, nature-narrative,
origin-extinction, entrance-exit. Out,

your fat tongue works once more.
We step into sunlight, midday's Oxford
traffic of flesh and thought, and hear:
"Everyday, till the day I die, I will always..."

*Emily Hasler*

# TO PENARTH PIER

It's the sky washed clean into the sea
and a stony shore where you hear
the world is falling to your right
in streamlets of gravel as you walk.

Signs of something before;
bold orange boulders
no natural beach would wear,
salt-wood and rusted piping.

You seek for larger pieces of the world
each foot stepping aching and cautious.
Finally it's a clamber to reach
the faded cheap charm.

Fit only for short stories
it's without a sense of history
of the fire and the crash withstood
of the structure's stand against

time and water and dancing you come.
Blinking windflown drops of sea
you picked a coast you don't know
to escape a city that will not have you.

The men will speak to you
if you smile, which you will
because the fat vinegary chips
are everything you ever wanted

and the sea is at your feet
making noises like someone
draining tea from a cup.
It has to end somewhere

but not here, on Penarth Pier
which was once much longer.

*Emily Hasler*

# COLD CALL

In the nightbound house, a phone rings.
It startles a puff of spores
from an orange whitening in the bowl.

Reverse charges from another spiral arm:
a voice without a body wants to talk,
it's asking for your middle name.

The stars are stammering a message
but their morse code will take
an accordion of universes to complete.

And when you throw your voice
through the open window, it too
will perish before it can reach

the one at the end of the garden
hunting by torchlight for the root of his tongue.

*Luke Heeley*

# LEAVING THE CINEMA IN DAYLIGHT

Fairytale years elapsed when
I climbed the velveteen stairway
for a season of back-row hibernation,
fading down to watch a widow
swimming length after length
in a subterranean pool.
Cancel that dream. I stumble out,
each cone and rod blown
by so many kliegs and *nuits Americaines*,
and breathe through my eyes, back
in the film that jitters through the gate
faster than anyone can direct:
MSG wafting from an alleyway vent,
the preacher's megaphone, convertible
thumping to the lights that switch
from green to red whether we're there or not.
The girl in the kiosk yawns.
She's waiting for her boyfriend to arrive
when the credits of the midnight show run out.

*Luke Heeley*

# LONDON PLANE TREE

Lung-negative, guardian of the minor road
where the codger rests for a moment
in his odyssey to the corner shop,
its digits examine the ins and outs
and register the ramifications.
Herald of the hump-back
where a fourth-hand Ford
grumbles by, it drags
on our exhaust and breathes back
balm for the scumbled moon;
and for this, while the good cop bad cop
of rain and snow interrogates its billboard bark,
it probes the lightlessness
for nourishment: the roots in rubbish.

*Luke Heeley*

# TO A NAUGAHYDE BOOTH

Your vinyl form engenders all the verbs:
to slide inside, lean back and meditate
within the kingdom of your window view
while slow-moving thoughts are born
in your jacuzzi of the mind
and milk billows in my coffee.

Darkness percolates in the saplings,
the motorway invisible except
for orange lamplight glow
beneath which drivers blink awake,
fast-lane micro-slumberers
drifting from their trajectory.

It's respite from traffic's breath I crave,
to be stilled as skin forgets velocity.
Let me defer the odometer and gauge
for the deviation of the chrome dispenser
from which serviettes are sprung
like doves from the magician's sleeve.

Remind me of how you exist beyond us,
along with concrete bunkers and sequoias
and the spliced beast that shed
your fabric strip by strip
before they set it free to gnaw forever
on a sofa flytipped in a ditch.

In the night of endless refills,
you receive any visitor's monologue or tranquility:
your studded frame a stronghold
for this time-lapse flicker
tantalised by the laminated menu's
knickerbocker glory with an extra maraschino.

*Luke Heeley*

## SAPPHIC: JAMESIAN, AUREATE

The Golden Bowl, you were,
    and I a crack
across that gorgeous patina.

Almost too much to break, to speak,
    disturb the dust
in a backstreet antique shop.

But you were something else
and something else again: a silence
    broken, after rain.

Where are you now? So bright, intense:
    O shining girl,
        my private Her,
the light that hammers every line.

*Jane Holland*

# AUDEN AND THE SUN

It is hard not to laugh
when you see the great poet
finding his balance atop
the world's tallest ladder
in a pair of dungarees —
indeed, it would be
downright foolish not to.

These are things to do with grief
as boxes are to do with moving house.

Imagine him; his face red
from all that sun and work
and tears and sweat, his paper
face puffing in the breeze
as he spanners the bolts free
and removes the supports,
slicing off wedges like cheese

As boxes are to do with moving house
these are things to do with grief.

And what does it mean
to drown yourself daily
in darkness? Here he comes
on feeble legs down the last
few struts at the foot, all that
sun on his back,
heavy as a black hole.

These are things to do with grief
as boxes are to do with moving house.

In a moment everything
can suddenly be gone
like a street where no-one is.
His paper face is blowing
round the vents in New York
as the subway rattles underneath
there is space in the air.

As boxes are to do with moving house
these are things to do with grief.

*Gavin Hudson*

# TO THE LIGHTHOUSE KEEPER

As the engine stalled into silence
somewhere near dawn, the boat became
tethered to the sea's devices and I
lay back on deck and felt the ocean writhe
beneath. You were passing me
palm over palm, wave over wave to reach
your shore over each shallow sandbank
between needle-sharp rocks. I listened
to the wet sounds the water made,
imagined our different positions in bed.
I counted each step up each stair you made
to the lamp room, found you fumbling matches.
I watched the wick bite at the flame
and the oil lit. The light singeing the crest
of each wave drawing me into your arms,
but the ocean was calm and I slept my way in.

*Gavin Hudson*

# CAMOUFLAGE

Savvy thin dog with the bleating ribs, dawn;
annunciation on the weekend lawn.

A comprehensible yap: "Am horny,
hungry, riddled with rage, shit-on-tawny.

I belch the taste of bone to the crisp skies,
I do not respond to name, to your cries."

Infants flog the garden rubble; paddling
pool inflates autonomously. Waddling

dog mooches into the dry plastic pond,
licks at a blue fish, its tongue like a wand

conjuring waterfalls from the creature's
unbidden brain. Laps at piscine features

delight a dirty baby, face of muck
and fun, garden a nebula to suck.

The season is besotted with small meals
like these potatoes. Invisible reels

of sunlight mythologise everything,
including the cold past, where the dead king

took the dog then put it back, burden of
strength. Hot stuff rays the survivor. A cough.

The garden disinvites the wraith of flesh;
it leaves the baby to its palace crèche.

Sky hangs its head, chin against the ridgy
spine of dogmeat, slinking sweat and midgy,

blood drying backwards. Memory of meat
is plastered on the brain, design of lunch

so real it floats and leaks juice over hind.
Dog, sleeping, opens its mouth and goes blind.

*Thom Hutchinson*


## TERMINAL DELIGHT

The notion that the small things might desire
and be desirable. There is immense
pleasure in not unreeling the wire
except if you are watched. And so the sense
like sherbert on the tongue – a sudden bomb
of love, or acceptance that love is possible.
Warm and fleet, every second some
sweet churn of effort. Or the weight of fossils
that occupy the crevice of soft hearts.
To tolerate the purchase of a bone
is simple. Buy the broken body, see
that you are understood by them, by me,
is sentiment. All one mistaken loan.
It isn't beautiful. You sell its parts.

*Thom Hutchinson*

# UNIFICATION

Cool welts on the staffer's arm
are divine intervention.
Sandwiches packed innocently

but the lettuce is off. Your
gesture
is appreciated, but sadly ruinous.

Enough audacity;
the day is thick enough,
thick with weather,

weather goosing the enduring
heritage
of palimpsestic digs.

(Roman prodding through the Tudor.)
His swollen skin;
his own child doing him in.

The Third Law
says I say this back to you.
Complaints about the rain today,

each season sings a quiet one.

*Thom Hutchinson*

# TURKISH DELIGHT

Uncle Mike had the shakes.
He couldn't hold things very well,
and when she poured his tea
she gave him a saucer and she didn't fill the mug.
Her mother must have told her this once
but now it was just something that she did.

Uncle Mike had the shakes
but being four she took the fact and left it there.
Some people had the shakes, some people couldn't walk,
there was a girl in her mother's class had six fingers on one hand.
These things are just things you know when you are four.

Sometimes Uncle Mike had the shakes so badly
he couldn't pick up things at all
and he went to stay in a big white house
like the hospital, but for heads
and her mother must have explained this the first time
and being four, she understood;
sometimes she had stories so badly she had to go and sit in the wardrobe
and write them down until her head was empty.

The thing she liked best about the head hospital
was the sweetie trolley
which always seemed to come around when they visited
and Uncle Mike liked to buy her things.
And once he bought her Turkish Delight
which was her favourite
[it was her mother's favourite]
and he opened it for her.

And the lady who pushed the sweetie trolley round
which seemed like a fun job
smiled at him and went away.
And she said thank you Uncle Mike
because her mother had told her once that was polite
and her mother smiled at him over her head and said
feeling better today then.

*Poppy James*

# OLD SKIN

the little man
who hand fed me olives
that were green with little red flecked pepper eyes
is still standing on my doorstep
twenty years after he left me for a sea green parrot.

this little man
keeps hopefully ringing my doorbell
but I am sitting under the letterbox
with parcels and postcards in my hair
and the hedgehog prickle of the doormat on my bottom
and I will not let him in.

he wants to share my bed
and shed his skin there
the skin he has been carefully saving
for twenty years for me

so that on the morning when the woman
he married instead of me
does not like him anymore
he can put his little ladder against the side of my bed
and climb in
to put it back on again
and trick me into loving him

this little man
has been standing on my doorstep for so long
that he has not noticed
his twenty years forgotten skin
has slipped down his legs like unbelted trousers
and I would like to pick it up and fold it into a suitcase
then leave the country
with him still standing on my doorstep
and his parrot swooping and shrieking in the sky.

*Poppy James*

# THE WASP CATCHER

If you break into his house
all you will find are spaces
where sofa, bed and tables ought to be.
A perfect carpet underneath its pristine plastic coat
and an empty kitchen bin.
The only thing he seems to own are
blue and unmarked plastic bags
all folded square and tucked away in drawers.
Perhaps that is when you would break back out and run.

The people in the cornershop sell polos
to a man who comes in late on Friday nights
he buys in bulk, still boxed, and wraps them up
in unmarked plastic blue, like children taking shells from beaches,
anticipating bumps.

He takes them home,
and you would be confused at his rows of perfect teeth
until the early hours of morning when he steps outside
and rips the paper down the tube of sweets
and lays the polos end to end along his windowsills.
He goes back in and locks the door
takes up his usual station on the floor, crosslegged,
and he waits.

With the first rays of sun, the wasps arrive,
in hundreds; each wasp claims a polo and it sets to work.
They eat into the sugar, from the middle out,
until what is left looks like a strip of lace,
and safe inside he watches.   It takes an average wasp
one day to eat its way around the loop.
The house hums, the walls will even move, with every tiny wingbeat
every bite.

Did you know some wasps are diabetic?
At night he goes outside
and with his little dustpan and its mismatching brush
and he sweeps away the bodies.

*Poppy James*

# FIVE-TO-NINE

it is always five-to-nine in this bed, always
five-to-nine as the other clocks chime and the air outside
travels between day and night, black to white.
it is always five to nine, when they bring me breakfast
always five-to-nine when they bring lunch
and *always* five-to-nine when I eat my dinner.
it was five-to-nine when his heart stopped, they say,
and it will be five-to-nine when I close my eyes
for the last time;
it will be as though we passed away in the same moment,
immortalised together in the atom of five-to-nine.
so let the other clocks chime and let the days pass,
and I will be content in this one minute world,
the three dimensions of these four walls
and the silent tick of my heart for company.

Sholeh Johnston

# BABIRUSA

Babirousa babyrussa
rustling and grubbing pork-like
in a sultana-wineskin hide.

Seam swollen.

Skinny thighs quibble under
the rootling bulk, buck digging
and chewing,
snoffling and coupling–
clicking the slate chops wetly.

Long lizard snout ratted,
balded, round on all edges.

Little sulawesi knees.

Fabled:
mud scaled and chuffing fatly
in the woodlouse woods.

Rolling in the bog flats or pittering
down the trip tracks
the little pig feet.

And low like a rhino, females
pick their slighter wrinkled rounds down
into Indonesian shades.

Slot yellow eyes pale as ewes
then ears, pointed
and tusks, pointed
curl through snouts like toenails
clipped sore from the stone-washed skin.

*Charlotte Jones*

# MOTH

They shoulder into the tongues of the gorse,
soft dusts shrugged by the points:
and the birch-bushes and bark-scapes
where the thick patterned tongues uncoil.
Wings wait in shade for dark,
shields shuddered under the stiff ribs of leaves,
the vein of petals,
the quiet sticks of autumn.
Night.
Fuzz-bodied they come and bead in strings round torchlight,
creeping through the little card catacombs
of the moth-trap. Egg box stacked, inviting dry:
The bacchic need for moon.
Crisp wings lose themselves silkily in their light lust.
Quivering, and they drowse,
quivering
And the soft fat drop of ice from roseberries
tremors like the half flight
of caught moths in morning:
Like a pin crunched frostily through the back of the head.

*Charlotte Jones*

# EARWIG

```
combs                          sentried
in her                          to wood
wings                           womb
  curvy                          eggs
    forceps                   moist
          to               her
           manipulate


                cerci


          The brood school
        around her leather hips
         learning how to climb
           into men's brains.
                Circe
       Your father was a sailor-wig
              she said
          Dr Beatty's assistant,
     crannied in his candle grease hair.
               Sorcerer
         curing Nelson's headache
         in a defensive freefall.
```

*Charlotte Jones*

# CUTTLEFISH

*The cuttlefish has eyes that develop before birth.*
*It begins observing whilst still in the egg,*
*and prefers to feed on prey it saw before hatching.*

Calcuim carbonate cuttlebones
unique to their buoyancy,
cast up on beaches.
Elsewhere they remain photochronic,
these chameleon-of-the-sea
whose strange eyes cannot see colour.

The Xenophores flash,
Erythrophores throb,
reflective Iridophores camoflage and communicate.
Cephlapodo arms reach out, colourful,
to the small mollusc prey,
denticulated suckers grasping through the sands.

Eight Cthulic limbs frill the sharp beak.
Three hearts beat independently
their green hemocyanin bloods.
The Kraken, hunting shrimp
with a mute intelligence.

The lucked-in child lifts his bucket to his face
Watching the tiny creature pulse through every repertoire
against the red plastic.
*Dolphin. Shark. Seal. Big Fish.*
It throbs,
but cannot hide from the pink fingers
so circles away into a puff of ink.

*Charlotte Jones*

## OH, YOU DON'T AGREE?

I don't want to sound like a prophet,
But last night I found over twenty things in Revelation
That could be metaphors for the internet.

I'm going to pretend I overheard that in Pret a Manger;
A pretty young mother said it to her baby son.
She ate a beef and watercress sandwich.

She said many beautiful and terrible things.
The smile of the ducks on his pram was beautiful
And terrible. All children are psychic.

I'm drinking this new red coffee, but then I swallow,
Hard. There is no red coffee. It doesn't exist.
Her long black coat is a tundra in profile. She says.

It's always sad in the alcoholic wing
When they wake up screaming,
'I saw Hell in a tomato! I saw Hell in a tomato!'

I too have seen Hell in a tomato.


## MINK FARM

Simon, I'm going to break the horizon over your head like a porcelain
baguette.
The house is a toy box from the old country - I mean the bad one.

My cat, Security Camera, knows every evil spirit by name.
A grey, beatific weekend; writers call requesting back-up:

'Trouble with poetry: the incandescent weirdos who hate you

Make up at least 10-20% of your audience, which is quite a market
share.

Small wonder most of us got sick of it and opened the mink farm.'
The minks are little misused apostrophes of teeth and cruelty.

I'd invite you to stay for dinner, but the only food in the house is an
egg-
Shell with a sad face drawn on shakily in biro and some old mustard
powder.

I think there's some bread in the... Oh. I must have eaten it.
The other people in my house check themselves out of bed like books.

I had little footnote numbers tatooed by my scars, 1 through 17.
Please refer to my "ass" or "butt" for full explanation.


## CRUMB TRAY

Miranda stands on the jetty knocking tennis balls into Lake Sensible.
She is wearing an Edwardian swimming costume, off-set with a jewel-
encrusted
Moth broach, engraved with: "This is way too much detail for *prose*,
even."

'The trouble with the first thought's felicity,' I say,
'Is what if your first thought is always to chop
Off your own feet and throw them over the park fence?'

Simon looks up from the broken toaster. 'I'm watching you,' he says.
'So don't even *think* about trying to chop off your own feet again.'
Simon is my case-worker. 'How's the case going, Simon?' I ask him.

'If that's an attempt at satire,' he says, shaking out the crumb tray.
Miranda has run out of tennis balls. 'I've just come up with a title
For Miranda's autobiography!' I annouce.

'If you're just going to let your thoughts run like that,'
Simon lines up eight tiny screws on the table and selects the first,
'Don't expect anyone else to be interested;

'At least try to off-set them with something mundane. A foil.'
Simon turns the screwdriver like he's operating a periscope.
'My approach to my thoughts is two-tiered,' I tell him,

'Like a cheap wedding cake. First, the way a saxophonist
Feels about their saliva looping out of the valve:
It's not strictly what my brain's *for*, but it's arrestingly unpleasant.'

We observe a minute's silence as Simon plugs in the toaster.
He fetches some bread. 'And the second tier?' he asks.
'Saxophonist Valve Unpleasant are *killer* endwords!' I say.


## 'MORE SAD NEWS FROM YOUR STUPID PLANET'

I make a cup of tea for each of the 68 cups in the house.
Given that matter cannot be created or destroyed,
Some of these cups must contain fragments of asteroid
From before the world began, which is amazing.

I arrange the cups of tea all over the ground floor.
When Simon arrives, I say, 'Hi Simon. Cup of tea?'
He's getting good; barely flinches. Picks up a cup.
Takes a sip. Sighs. 'You may be batshit crazy,' he says,

'But you certainly make a good cup of tea.'
Between us we drink every single cup. I am beginning
To like Simon, his courteous smile like a weak
Line-break, the fashionable cut of his jaw-line.

Miranda is out on the Vesper delivering death threats.
"*This is just more sad news from your stupid planet.*"
She is the most private, ecstatic, non-confrontational
Person I have ever met. She owns several parasols.

Everything has been so, so wonderful today
I think I am going to drink some poison and not be killed by it!
But then it's back to the A&E for grim smiles, clipboards,
Ammonia smell, green walls, machines.

'Trouble is,' I explain to Simon before they ask me to count to ten.
'I'm so insecure I can't stand to hear anyone else complimented.
Even for something in which I have no interest.
If you said, *Herman is the best mountain climber I've ever met*,

I'd secretly resent Herman. I'd be like, *And what am I?*
*Chopped liver? Am I some chopped liver trying to climb*
*A mountain? Flubbing onto the snowy rocks and partially freezing*
*On the underside? Picked at by huskies? Mountain doves?*

But then I apologise for sounding all weird.
I am worried that Simon might be fired
Because I drank the poison on his watch,
So I call my notary public and have him witness

The following statement at my bedside:
'I didn't drink the poison because I was sad:
I drank it because I was too happy!'
And he writes it down, verbatim:

I DIDN'T DRINK POISON BECAUSE I WAS SAD,
I DRANK IT BECAUSE I WAS TOO HAPPY.
'Maybe an exclamation mark,' I murmur.
He disagrees. 'Where's Miranda?' I ask.

'She practically *is* an exclamation mark;
She'd understand. One... Two... Three... Four...'
Unconsciousness like an apple falling into a bowl of soup.
An apple thrown out of a mirror and caught, off-screen.
I am reminded of a detective story:

A detective was hired to find a tiny bead.
That's pretty much the end.

He dedicated his whole life to the search,
Ruining his posture and eyesight.

After nearly twenty years, the detective,
An old man by this point in the story,

Found the bead in a carpet showroom.
His hand trembling, he picked it up,

Took it to the man who had hired him
To find that he had died eight years ago.

Chicken-wire ruins pilgrimages:
There is nothing so untransfigured.

It's like trying to write with someone
Looking over your shoulder:

The only thing you can think to write is:
*Will you stop looking over my shoulder?*


FARFALLE *or* THE ARGUMENT

The wood pigeons become increasingly irate:
"Your *child*-ren hate you!
Your *unc*-les hate you!
Your *doc*-tor hates you!
Your *bar*-ber hates you!"

Miranda is re-arranging the craft box.
'We're going to have a regime change,'
She says, distressingly breezy.
'You're to make something every day
And evaluate it in your craft journal.

I make a noise like a distant car.
I make a bow-tie by threading a piece
Of *farfalle* onto a some string.
I colour it in with a black marker.
I evaluate it: "Disappointing."

"Too many poems addressed to much better artworks,
Too many poems addressed to much better writers.
*Oh, Borges, I take off my hat to you,*
*A hat filled with a million libraries,* etc.
Let's at least agree that's bullshit."

That's what I write in my journal.
Miranda is wearing fortune-teller chic.
'It's a start, I suppose,' she says.
'You would tell me?' I check with her.
'If you didn't like it, I mean.'

Simon enters the room. He wears a jumper
Embroidered with the face of a complete stranger.
'Who's that?' I ask him.
'I don't know,' says Simon.
Miranda lights a cigarette and stares at him.

'We're going to have an argument,' she says.
'On July the 14th. I'm not going to tell you
What it's about.' Simon walks in a little circle.
He starts pulling his own hair.
'You *always DO* this,' he says.

'How can you just carry on like
Nothing's wrong for *two months?*'
'I don't feel like talking about it yet.'
'A HINT? Can you at least give me a hint?'
'No,' says Miranda, 'sorry.'

'I hate you, Miranda,' says Simon, in tears.
The pigeon says, "Your *girl*-friend hates you!"
'I hate you so much.' (I ask Simon if he likes my bow-tie,
If he gets the analogy, but he waves me off).
'Save the waterworks for the argument,' suggests Miranda.


## THE BEAUTIFUL NECKLACE OF SELF-DENIAL

I'm so modest I've been handing out
Someone else's business cards for the last five years.

In the mail I learn that Patrick V. Cane has died
(Weather vane, loose tile) and that I'm to stop.

'My problem with the Shepherd of Hermas,' I say,
Mouthful of bolognese, 'is, you know, what was so great

About his accuser? We're supposed to believe that *she*
Never entertained an impure thought?

And anyway, I thought we weren't supposed to judge.
It's like all of the riches and treasures analogies:

I thought we weren't supposed to care about that shit.
So why sell us all the self-denial stuff

Using riches and treasures analogies?
"The lovely and really expensive earrings of renunciation."

It seems patronising.'
'Someone's chirpily irreverent this morning,' says Simon.

'Trouble is you're either going to take everything as a punishment from God,
(Including stepping on a thumb-tack),

*Or* you're just coming up with the second half of the metaphor before the first,
Which is to say the analogy before the thing itself:

Like a… I don't know.
I can't remember what I was talking about.'


'The homeopathic cure for insomnia is a one-man-band.'
Says Miranda. 'And vice versa.'


## I'LL DIE IF YOU DISTRACT ME

The activist has been put to death
He had proven himself untrustworthy by informing on his father
For holding a secret reading group in the family basement.
At first the commissioner was delighted by this,
But then he started thinking, 'How far can you trust a man…'

This is a day of joy and terror for everyone,
Yet I feel like my chest is covered in flat pebbles;
Like someone I respect just showed me porn on their mobile phone.
Where is the despair artist? The delicatessen.
I watch Simon playing a retro computer game:

Tended by fireflies, the thug bathes in a waterfall of natural ink.
'I'm sorry I'm not much of a human being!' he calls.
'That's okay!' we yell from our chalk-white houses.
The fireflies bring him breadcrumbs, one by one
Until he has eaten a whole loaf of bread.

'This is the best game ever!' I exclaim.
'Quiet!' says Simon, 'I'll die if you distract me.'
I go back to my slim volume. But then I look up.
'Can anyone actually give me a convincing answer
As to why e. e. cummings didn't use capital letters?'

I say. 'Don't give me that anti-authority crap, either.'
Silence. Simon continues feeding breadcrumbs
To the bathing thug. 'Any thoughts?' I say.
'Actually I read his autobiography,' says Miranda.
'Turns out the SHIFT button was busted on his typewriter.'


EYES

Miranda has overshot the picture-hook budget by £7,000.
Simon just says, 'Well, they *are* really beautiful picture-hooks;

It almost seems a shame to hang pictures on them.'
He is trying to shore up some points for the argument in July.

I have my hands on my shoulders, examining my elbows' flat planes.
'You see how like the desert they are?' Miranda says.

'There's the hermitage, and, between your elbows, the ravine.
The golfcourse is that patch of psoriasis.'

'And that goose-bump must be the hermitologist's mound!'
I exclaim, but Miranda snorts into her Margarita.

'Yeah, right,' she says. '"Hermitologist"!'
Simon says, 'You shouldn't confuse the world with your elbow.

'Rather see the world as a planet-shaped horse:
It gallops faster the more you beat it

With the undersides of your feet.'
'That may be all very well for you,' says Miranda.

'But then you hang around with people whose favourite
Metaphor for "eyes" is "porn spoons" -

As in, "Get yer porn spoons into that!"
Or, "Cor, that's a sight for sore porn spoons!"'

Simon is playing an imaginary computer game.
He sits in front of the blank kitchen wall

Wildly fiddling with a control pad. He says to me,
'You'd better start thinking about wrapping it up now.'

'The present?' I indicate the toy robot on the microwave.
'No,' says Simon. 'Not the present.'


ELIJAH

Miranda has been studying International Relations
In secret and has now fled for Bangladesh with the UN.
'All beautiful women think they can save the world,'
Scoffs Simon. 'It's a standard attendant pathology.'
She leaves behind: some soap with a bee in it;
A purple wrap around dress with small nail varnish stain;
A giant hat box containing a hat the size of a 50p piece;
An unopened packet of menthol flavoured Marlboroughs;
Seven International Relations text books and a Bible;
A champagne cork decorated to look like a little soldier;
A DVD copy of a Swedish zombie film called *Död Vandrande*;
A camera with a half used film and her tax return.
I arrange these effects in the shape of Miranda.
I lie face down on it like Elijah and start crying.

*Luke Kennard*

# THE LOST COMPASSES

lying low
in shuffled mounds
are lost
compasses
abandoned
to the ground
gloveless
grasses shiver
through the sun's
splintering foam
they taste the
rising river
of frost and
fall asleep
beneath the snow
but the lost
compasses
abandoned
to the ground
sink to nothing
are never found

*Gwenfron Kent*

# MORONIC GHAZAL

I'm going to love you absolutely, like an absolute moron.
I'll waste my life counting your teeth with my tongue, like a moron

I'll spend days waiting for your image on a black and white CCTV
monitor.
I'll always expect you in colour and I will always be a moron.

I'm going to kiss bits of air where I've seen you standing
until I catch something that distinguishes me as a sick little moron.

I'm going to take photographs of things I'm sure we must both have seen
To remind me of the world we share in common. To remind me I'm a
moron.

I'm going to scream your name until we both forget what it means
so I can recast you in soft sounds like a self satisfied moron.

I'm going to frame the calendar pages from days I bump into you
and entitle the portfolio *My Favourite Year: The Entire Life's Work of A Moron*

I'm going to replace the national anthem with your ring tone
because I'd rather be talking to you than belong to a moron.

I dream of the day I have enough self esteem to dream about you.
I've bought sleeping pills in bulk. I'm fully prepared to be a moron.

I'm going to remember you in my final will and testament
Even if, God forbid, you die first. I will be forever the moron.

*Will Kerr*

THE POET ATTEMPTS TO ADVISE HIS YOUNGEST BROTHER IN
THE ART OF LIVING AS A SICKNESS RISES THROUGH HIM AND
THE WHOLE WORLD DISTORTS IN THE MANNER OF A
PROJECTION, SKEWED AT SOURCE BY THE FUMBLING HANDS
OF UNKNOWN LOVERS, OR ELSE DROWNED OUT BY THE
FIRES OF THEIR EYES.

Our spending of twenty seven hours straight
trying to locate Tracy Island on Google Earth
was not a waste of time.

Do not, however,
ever let me catch you smoking,
telling the truth or falling in love.

*Will Kerr*

# WE, MUDLARKS

Official – yes, and paid: not in traded
fruit and meat, or pickled loot, or even
on commission. An actual, annual wage!
Stapled to signed, certificated permission

from the *County Council*.

Next time the cold comes – the watermouth
yawns frost upstream, cackle-casing
the barge-bed in unspadeable peaks of lace
and glass – I mean to found a Union:

Of Archdeacons, Locksmiths & Blacksmiths.
Of Harbour-Masters, Haberdashers &, ideally
speaking, Cobblers (although I fear the Ronnie
Barker, smells-like-a-hardware-store appeal

of * SHOE REPAIRS * signs

has clubbed that most edible of shopfront
words into a thickly Ronsealed strongand
-silence). Of working-men of *Title* – only
we won't use 'Union'; we'll prefer 'Guild'.

And Aldermen of all of this, we shall stand,
framed permits hung between our hands:
we, Murdlarks! Stained from groin to toe
with silt and wet and frog and treasure.

We, Mudlarks! Less Indiana Joneses
of the riverbank then Boba fucking Fetts. We,
Mudlarks! Princes of the pale space that sees
eccentricity bubble into the downright deceptive.

For birds we are not.

*Sam Kinchin-Smith*

At least there is food for their wintering.
She holds the few he found when he kicked at the soil,
and rubs at the yellow paper-skin. They smell of nothing.
Just the earth, she thinks. Where they have come from.
They are like lovers in their flourishing.
Some have chosen the North, where the days are long.
Their bulbs crouch beneath the surface,
tight and pale as the skull of a vole,
greedy for the light that warms them.
Others prefer the mild winters of the South; short days,
more time for the quietness of one another,
and for contemplation in the dark.
Their bulbs will be bitter at harvest –
They will not give of themselves lightly.
Then the frost, the child of Winter banging its tambourine.
Other vegetables, half-formed, are crystallised in the earth.
Allium Cepa survives, as one does.

When the sky turns white as the ground –
the trees and hedgerows tired and shy and tense
in their patience for Spring, their outwitting of Winter –
and the pantry is full of this harvest only,
it is a meagre food.
The lovers at the table count the days
until the prediction of the last frost.
A month before, they will venture out
to plant more – perhaps bulbs or seeds.
They will be wrapped in wool and thick with the smell of one another.
They will push the rusted metal of the spades they forgot about
beneath the frosted topsoil. They will till the earth,
the thrust of their hands like dancers,
until they uncover the dark, chill earth a few inches below,
where the onions will grow.
The act of burial is not lost on them.
They will press the earth back into place, gently,
and retire to the house. She will boil the water

that he has broken from the frozen well,
and fry the onions until they give up their bitterness,
the way Winter gives way to Spring.

*Anna Lea*

# UNDER A MOROCCAN SKY

The desert frozen air
of the night in Marrakesh
breaks only for the
sun that is summoned
when the preacher of the mosque
with his tongue pulls the words
of God from the sky
and puts them in my ears
and throws them at the night
till the stars fade to light
and the moon catches fire
while bundled in blankets
on a terrace on a roof
as those words take flight
and the day uncurls
beneath the new sun
we speak the prayer together
of all gods and none.

*Tim Leach*

## 'UNKNOWN ROAD'

This is my corner of the Winster Valley.
Many have questioned it as they drive past.
Where I stumble home intoxicated
with my adulterous neighbour. Just for the crack.

This is home of my gentle steps
that grow older and older,
taller - perhaps not much taller.
My blonde hair dirtied with passing years

This is where I think the most.
Imagine all those conversations,
the friend of a friend and the school heartthrob.
Talk to myself. It is purely silent.

Winter: the only noise is the rustling of pheasants
set for idyllic roosting; roasting.
Summer, it itches my eyes. Grass.
Hay balls that dance past my eyebrows.

There are the times
I'll kick at its ground
as I stack it in stupid shoes, on one of its many pot-holes
or throw my weight at it in temper.

My place.
I cry to it.
When know one will listen,
confess all that I don't even want to hear.

This is my place.
Break between world and home and tradition,
envelops me for five minutes
before I hit the noise again.

This is the place that drowns
my toes in April showers.
Rain. Always rains.
But allows me to leave footprints

in the cold, sheltered dry of the trees,
in the dry of the sun,
in the constant knowing that each step is ours
—It remembers me too.

*Emma Lowe*

# ICE PALACE

Outside there is an ice palace
the men of the city have carved
in the city square.
Their coatless backs are drawn up high
to lift the ice, and seem to us quite
inexplicably blue
through the shimmer of the gable walls.
If it were not for the pull of their eyes
under such dark and forceful brows
their shapes would float, undisturbed,
like nár-corpses in the water.
It is not hard to think how
the roof must bear upon the heads of those men
with the weight of old artic ice
almost opaque but for the low sloped pediments
rising into points of translucency.
Greened bronze figures lean in and consider
like tusks their own wavering counterparts,
who seem to own the cleanness of old
undiscovered caves.
The men from the desert and the steppe
stand close and want to press their palms
into the bricks. The light of such a shallow
sideways sun makes walls turn to clear jellied air
and all the young men do is doff their hats
beckoning to one another
apparently forgetful of the snow.

It occurs to me that
they should house some rare specimen in the ice,
pale creatures set, iridescent and unmoving
in each blue architrave. I cannot help but see its rooms
populated with grotesque rubber flesh,
some tiny-eyed colossal squid.
They would have to trawl its frozen hulking mass
ebony beak clacking, up from the south
its bizarre arms stretching on forever
the warm currents reworking layers of blood-flushed red.
Yet now the snow-dirt clings to our mammalian heat,
to the walls of our great buildings
and the horses, ducking in their harness;
appear as triangle of three
swinging their heads in an eerie troika.

*Ailie MacDonald*

# A LIGHT WELL

The road where you live has no streetlights
and when you turn off the lamp it is darker
than I have known in a long time.
I can no longer see you, or the room where you
have never settled and which looks as if
you could be preparing to leave it for good.

The alarm's ticking is loud and rapid;
the phone rings long after midnight
and no one is there. You won't sleep
on your left side, afraid to hear your heart
and all night I am on the wrong side of you.
There is an art to this, or a compromise.

The room emerges as the light thickens
behind the blind; the shape of things
that never left: your photographs
filling the gaps on the walls like plants
growing into a light well. Slow to wake,
we yawn and dress; fall asleep on the train.

Liz Manuel

# FEBRUARY'S ICE

The cobbles furred with frost and the early start
a shock, on what seemed like the coldest
day of the year. The winter was flanked
by our reunions, each one an equinox
as we closed distance and balanced our lives.

We were not alone the second time
and the crowd of us joined a walking tour
that took us alongside tall, shuttered houses,
through chilled open spaces and across water
held still by ice at its core. In the pictures
our lime white faces are caught
in sun that split through mist from the canals.

On the way home, through back streets,
lights burnt from windows covered with red curtains.

*Liz Manuel*

# GLASS HOUSE MOUNTAINS

The wide, baked main road, leading
to a wide, baked railway, is lined with a strip
of drying grass, where residents have left
their scrap metal for collection:

parts of cars, a cooker, an ironing board
with rust the same colour as the dirt.
Left there for a man who never arrived,
who chose instead to follow the road

away to the mountains that defy
the elegance of their name. He left
behind him the town's schoolchildren
who ask for the time, then ask again;

hearing a new accent they want to try out,
probing the vowels in *quarter to four*.
They make glass house eyes at a tourist
who has come far for nothing to see

and who won't guess that their curiosity
is more than his tourist imagination can hold,
as they stare down while walking their bikes
across the width of the bridge, again and again.

*Liz Manuel*

# I LOVE MY LOVE WHEN LOVERS TOUCH

I prefer it when she lets me
Rest my head upon her shoulders
My ear entangled in her tousled hair.
I like to hear the whispers from
Every tip, every split end
Telling me stories of
The long, slow, downwards journey they have spent
One close voyage, growing steadily away.

I like to return
To the contours of her face
Old, explored, familiar territory.
My fingertips probe each echo of flesh
Each ripple and crevice,
Eyes clamped shut so blemishes
The compass of the eyes
Do not perturb my oil painting.
I feel the ruby of her lips
Stain onto my fingers.

I feel it best, when we embrace,
My hands seep through her back
When clutched so tight her bones decalcify
And spread, like silver nitrate
Until I forget where body stops and feel
Like I can probe through her insides
Revealing something that
My longing fingers can relate to
Something they can grasp
And squeeze, and feel a part of.

And when we ripen
When grey becomes our predominant colour,
When liver spots and cracked blood vessels
Mottle out maps on the backs of our hands
Let me grasp yours closed in mine.
Let my failing fingers slide between
The bulwarks of your swollen useless knuckles,
Let me feel your paunchy, sagging palm
Clutched against mine.
And that will be enough.
And I will be happy.

*Jack McGowan*

# THE CYCLING GEOLOGIST
*Grenville Arthur James Cole (1859-1924)*

Excursion 1: The Gypsy Road

Poland first, and the minerals of Myslenice,
then across the alluvial plains, and up through
the Tatra mountains, Grenville on the three-wheeled
Humber-Beeston, Gerald Butler in the crow's nest,
the old penny-farthing, keeping a fair speed, cutting
through limestone, a curious couple, unused to the heat,
unused to the local uses of language, when to speak German
and when to speak English, and when either would see a slammed door.
With the help of strong thighs they entered the Alps,
cooled tired muscles in the river at Garam,
stopped off to see the mines at Hajnik, at Schopferstollen
ran fingers across the silver, two Slovakian boys
holding the lanterns, beaming at payment, then
the cone at Schladnigberg, and the burning coals
near Dux (*Oligocene, Miocene*), burning, still
and always burning – how he found the time to note
the sediments, scribble down his verses on volcanoes,
collect and store the fragments for his students –
one thousand and fifty miles in thirty-eight days,
Krakow to Coblentz, the legs turning, the tinkle
of stones in the spokes, the odd whirr of wheels
startling horses. You can never imagine a grimace,
a face strained at a hill, but it must have been there.
Instead there is only the thought of him smiling,
free-wheeling past olive groves, leaning back his sun-hatted head
and shouting to Butler in the gods: 'It is wonderful
what amount of rock has to be cut away before
you can make a decently artistic mountain.'

Excursion 2: *As We Ride*

It had been her idea to cycle down the aisle,
and Grenville, still so much her tutor, had agreed;
it was like they'd cycled from the church and never stopped,
honeymoon turned lifelong expedition, France, Germany,
Poland and the Balkans, and Ireland too, her homeland
and his home. What he made of rocks she made of people:
cold and brittle, overwhelming, or, uniquely interesting,
made with the sort of edge that will take three years
to understand, such time to stop not known on their itinerary.
Sometimes they grew tired.
There is a photograph of her, circa 1900, sheltering
beneath a tree, her head resting in her hands, fed up,
watching her husband pull off his boot, their bikes
stacked on the verge. But she fell in love with Orahova,
and so did he, the small town deep between iced mountains,
the name they chose for their home in Carrickmines.

Excursion 3: Ireland Student Trip 1903

*Dalradian, Silurian, Carboniferous.*
It was an unknown language for the west,
a queer way to talk of Mayo, the gristly bogs
of Galway. The boys made notes studiously,
and one stopped to snap the teacher's 'Roadster'
beneath Croagh Patrick, or maybe he snapped it
himself, the tool of the new evangelism, funded
by the State, peddling talk of millions
east through Omagh, under Slieve Gallion
to the Antrim Plateau – *gneissic, Tertiary, Cretaceous.*
They rooted around in Kilroot for salts from the Triassic,
then belted down to Belfast to chip off basalt
from Cave Hill, and on the last day, up at the crack
of dawn, they scaled Slieve Donard, watched the light
moving barren and brown across the Mournes.
Oh for a last free-wheel, he thought, his legs
beginning to seize, his hands locked tight
on the bars, (the funding stopped).
Oh for another hundred million years of cycling!
    A zip down
mountains with the wind moaning softly in the pass.

*Michael McKimm*

# TIERCE DE PICARDIE

She stumbles in heels, foal clip-clopping,
willow legs shaking, something on her top

that could be vomit. I can see her knickers
and her back-fat; the skirt is too short

and she is too young. He is too old:
he stumbles with plastic bag and broken

trainers across the road, something on his
trousers that could be piss. The children are fat

and loud: the mother runs after one and leaves
the baby crying in the pushchair in the street.

The group of boys pitches a burger against
our door, the clothes their mothers bought

them creased and stained; they are too young
for washing and washing up. I watch them all

from my window, seeking the clue which will
help me understand them. I have done this night

and day for a whole year, from my corner high-up
room, apart and above, within and looking out –

and I have loved this town like nowhere else.

*Jennifer McLean*

# IN YOUR COMPANY

I spend all the time I'm with you, trying
Not to wish I were somewhere else, when you
Make those ridiculous comments or laugh
At something unfunny. This is not what
I imagined growing up meant, knowing
When to keep silent, pick at my fingers
And smile inanely, sublimating all
The unworthy thoughts I have into a
Crystalline hypocrisy. And your views
Are disgusting and your habits are worse,
And it worries me that you brought me up
When my mum was busy. I am your blood
And bone and everything I am is you,
And in fifty years or so I can quite believe
I will have become you, although the thought
Terrifies me. And I am truly sorry
That I've always thought you were quite stupid,
And that I'll be better off without my
Accent, and that I've never had any
Sympathy over what your father did.
How much of my withholding do you see?
I've wondered if you were listening so
Often that I forget how much you hear.
It upsets me that I'll never tell you
About so many things that bear me up
And cast me down, because you wouldn't care
Or understand, or even disapprove.
You always talk about when I was young,
And I hate to hear it, hoping always
To erase you, or change you, or love you.
I love you. I don't love you. I love you.
When you're dead I'm sure I will cry for days.

*Jennifer McLean*

## YOU SEVEN

When you battle the sheets and heave a bedroom window
stars are sliding up from no horizon:
there are seven of you with wings because you heard me
      no other reason.

Togetherness you comment on in the daytime
you always want to be the last to mention
but you're always somehow first, so the ice you stand on
      stays unbroken.

Did you mention time has stopped for us? I believe
you mentioned time has stopped for you. 'Causation?
don't get me started!' you start saying to no one'
      but one and she didn't listen.

You fell so long ago, you catch their eyes
the other six, twelve eyes then zero eyes as
twelve eyelids close like day and the falling angels
      fall in sun-shades.

When you battle the sheets and hoist a bedroom window
stars are zooming up from no horizon.
You try to rise again, sit up so quickly
      they're snapped like children

stock-still in the sky but What's The Time,
Mr Wolf has rules the opposite
and you're not remotely quick enough and it's cloudy
and to hell with it.

You fell so long ago, the things you did
aren't written down, a digest of your crimes
would make a baby shrug and they don't do that;
      mutter your seven names

and actually, sorry, that wouldn't mean a thing.
Did you mention time has stopped for you? You did
but your fourteen eyes mist over at the words
  *for you* and I am afraid

I am going to have to go. Also you act
like time made a decision. Something broken
hasn't decided that. Don't get me started
  you say but no one

does. There are 7 of you, that's the digit
points you into the world, one holy plateau,
a downward slash forever, you can call that
  seven if it saves you.

*Glyn Maxwell*

## COMFORTLESS NOISE
*For Eilish*

"What kind of line does
the horizon slice?
Stippled closest and
white far off."

What are they saying?
If she can make it out
it can fill today's date
on the calendar.

Youngest is a heartbreaker,
but who does *she* look
like? Her mother's
mother perhaps. She's

fierce, looks very
like herself.
Now I know them.
I know them now.

"It's a long road from Carndonagh.
When it's time to leave
we can say it was lovely to
see her looking so well."

*Peter Maxwell*

# SAPPHO

Frankly, I wished he'd
gone, he strung it out for too long,

when he'd left, I laughed
out loud then

sung to my budgie.
Remember, my budgie,

the time you sat on my shoulder
and we danced around the

kitchen; you said
"it's ok Jenni,

he's gone now,
we don't have to make

polite conversations about
ivy crowns and

dancing in woods."

*Jennifer Mellor*

# CAMARGUES

*I will wake up in a world that hooves have led to*  Les Murray

Some horses are caves; you catch
that by the way they flicker and shy
at shadow. You can walk inside horses
and sense their walls trembling around you.
Camargues are air-delvers, the pile-driver
we're gripping on our reins, chiselling
granite miles. We caught their backs like luck
then held on. Camargues are not cave,
but they passed through like wraiths
slamming silently through the walls.

Thug-faced, hog-necked, anvil-hoofed
Camargues—necking the paint's hay
on cave walls of Niaux and Lascaux;
cantering behind the wasted warriors
of Rome, Persia and Greece. We rode
them here—or they rode us, chests thumped
out like wagons heaving our wagons;
warmed to our genius grandfathers
because they whispered to them
in horse and only in horse.

We should as well cremate ourselves
alongside our Camargues, riding them
through heaven's walls, hoofed pyres
to our Saints Mary Jacobe and Mary Salome.
We might have fired our horses
on our deaths as we fired our houses;
burnt ourselves upon the deaths
of our horses since we were their houses.
All horses are spells, but Camargues
are myth. You catch that on horseback.

*David Morley*

# CHORUS
## on the birth of Edward Daniel Keenan Morley

The song-thrush slams down gauntlets on its snail-anvil.
The nightjar murmurs in nightmare. The dawn is the chorus.
The bittern blasts the mists wide with a booming foghorn.
The nuthatch nails another hatch shut. The dawn is the chorus.
The merlin bowls a boomerang over bracken then catches it.
The capercaillie uncorks its bottled throat. The dawn is the chorus.
The treecreeper tips the trees upside down to trick out insects.
The sparrow sorts spare parts on a pavement. The dawn is the chorus.
The hoopoe hoops rainbows over the heath and hedgerows.
The wren runs rings through its throat. The dawn is the chorus.
The turnstones do precisely what is asked of them by name.
The wryneck and stonechats also. The dawn is the chorus.
The buzzards mew and mount up on the thermal's thermometer.
The smew slide on shy woodland water. The dawn is the chorus.
The heron hangs its head before hurling down its guillotine.
The tern twists on tines of two sprung wings. The dawn is the chorus.
The eider shreds its pillows, releases snow flurry after snow flurry.
The avocet unclasps its compass-points. The dawn is the chorus.
The swallow unmakes the Spring and names the Summer.
The swift sleeps only when it's dead. The dawn is the chorus.
The bullfinches feather-fight the birdbath into a bloodbath.
The wagtail wags a wand then vanishes. The dawn is the chorus.
The corncrake zips its comb on its expert fingertip.
The robin blinks at you for breakfast. The dawn is the chorus.
The rook roots into roadkill for the heart and the hardware.
The tawny owl wakes us to our widowhood. The dawn is the chorus.
The dawn is completely composed. The pens of its beaks are dry.
Day will never sound the same, nor night know which song wakes her.

*David Morley*

# MAIDEN IN THE MAP: 1610

Here's the place. Stand still. She is not hard to find:
Speed has spread a lacework of lanes over
the Amazon curves of my lover, who turns on waking.
Her legs are crossed at White Fryers,
her hip rests on Grayfriars Gate
and the wall at Gosford Streete runs
a hand along her ass; then she slackens
Fleete Streete's leather bond
strapping one breast to a necklace of rivers
saying St Michael's is her navel
but a School throngs at her heart —
and reclines below me on a throw of the Chilesmore meadows
where I am dizzy as the samphire gatherer hanging
with basket to a chalk cliff, the folio not yet printed.

*Jonathan Morley*

upstairs your mingle mangle
leathery books
fingertip-soft pages
and your voice at last

*they that thirle or boare throughs perles*

in the vault
handwriting craves
to long swaying lines
on curling     yellow like bark the parchment shores

*to eye a woman wiftly     as having a wanton desire to her*

stone heads     scratchd names
scripts neat
crabbed
broke

   *lurcher or devourer*
*the slit or clist in the neb of a penne*

a life preserved in a Lexicon
LATINO-ANGLICI PARALIPOMENA

*hoarie full of grey haires*
*the pan seethes and wallops*
*God send you many scholars*
*to bubble or cast up bubbles as urine in the urinal*

mine

*inward and hollow writhing the hair crisped curled artificially*
 *wax lither and hartlesse*
*a pedlar or one that hucketh*
*when in anger teeth dash gnash one against another*

   all my paines hath beene
    to purge it from infinite absurdities
     committed in precedent impressions

*Jonathan Morley*

# COVENTRY BOYS

One pie-shaped boy
in sky-blue T
jumps from the car's
passenger door
to flob on bus
while his father's
hid by the bus:
almost knocks me

three rat-face boys
playing cricket:
foot-length of dowel
fistful of gravel
end of the road

six little Sikhs
pelt like foals
uphill from Swanswell:
their heads are boats
the sky scrap metal

*

name
Arthur Genders
Builders Merchants
off Clovelly Row
Kev's Chop Shop
Beautiful Cuticles
The Kurdistan Hand Car Wash
Moira's Wet Fish
the city names
the sanctuary
of those who turn the lathes
those who drive the buses
those who make fins
to spin the propellers

that fly the jet engines
rolling the king
back to his boys
those who make screws
of certain length
and are sold along
with their machine
those who mend
great leather belt
hundreds of yards
on the factory floor
to synchronise the men
the screeching and strafing of metal
thing strange in these days

      *

I'll take you bab up the Ollybrush Balti
and I will buy you chicken jahlfrezi,
we'll listen to the radio all night long
its mingle of Bollywood and Quran
and I'll ignore the intercom's commands
for your eyelashes curl like their melodies:
the only way to travel, beetling down
the Hill, the drilling engine shouts to roar
then we're swooping like Whittle on the town,
panels shaking, the tom-tom's crosshair
trained upon the point our chariot was born
as precise as German radio-beams
flickring along our moonlit rivers:
the Burges— the Birdcage— the Campbell— Club Release—
and what of the abuse, the vomit-stained
seat, quick-legged lads in the entryway, the
Poles encroaching on the licensed strip?
I carry a kirpan, and at my call
each sore-arsed cabby in the Foleshill Road
shall be at my back, nimbler than the police
whose cast-off gadgets our quick sons can doctor.

*Jonathan Morley*

# RADAGAST THE BIRD-TAMER

Dogs are to be given the gift of eggs,
it's there in black and white. The *Telegraph*
omits that, this Easter, a TV chef
alerted the nation to the fact half
our kids don't know an apple from a leek,
they're growing up malnourished and brain-dead
but let's feed dogs an egg a day— poached eggs,
for brighter teeth and hair than some girl-chav
in a Council flat. Warwickshire farmers,
the quality and surplus of their food,
their kindness to animals. My eyes fail.

Old painter, teacher, Punglish-speaker, beard
nest to escaped songbirds from Stow Fair, go,
wassail your cider-trees; make our sap burn.

*Jonathan Morley*

# EXPLORATION
*After Elizabeth Bishop*


*Computer*


Between ten and twenty million years ago,
the eastern subcontinent collided with the
larger western continent. The eastern plate
continued to move westwards, displacing
continental crust and uplifting this chain of
high black mountains.


*Keyboard*


The central plain is dominated by post-glacial
geographic features. Steep moraines and the
oily scoop of low drumlins feature alongside
gnashing eskers, fatty kames and the plunging
grey of the kettle holes. Aerial reconnaissance
reveals  the industry of the native people;
does white denote a morgue?


*Books*


These then are the poor dead presidents,
coping a desert yardang squat.


*Pens*


Initially reports suggested this structure was part
of an advanced space programme. But we know
now that such a principality never possessed the funds
or the technology. It is larger than the
Matterhorn. We must provide it with a larger name.

*Mirror*

The question: where are the people of this land?
All the evidence suggests that they were once prosperous.
The answer: they stood before this sky. It was not blue.
It showed them twice as many hands, and legs and shoulders
than they had imagined. Believing in their doubleness,
they wore themselves to death building a great city.
It is now nothing more than a watermark in the north.

*John Murray*

Paint us, they said, the world as it is. No more
of your children's games and peasant weddings.
He painted *Procession to Calvary*, Saul
blasted by glory on the way to Damascus. At home,
now, transposing Holy Land to his own

familiar yellows, he did *Adoration of the Kings,*
in snow. He was good at snow. Go on
they said. He did *Flight into Egypt*,
a *Census at Bethlehem*, branchy veins
down a red hound's legs.

Not one was satisfied. He made smoke
like dry ice lift over a maimed chandelier
in rubble just that shade of dun we see
night after night on TV
in a totally annihilated village.

There are bodies in there, he said. Forty
disabled kids with their mothers
you can't see. And a Beirut reporter.
That's more like it, they said. We want
the world we live in. He painted *Slaughter*

*of the Innocents* (putting them too in snow,
and three hundred thousand refugees
in a red and black landscape).
Not hell, but it could have been.
From a plasma screen

he painted a boy of twelve,
his mouth that black egg-timer mask
of Tragedy, plastered crimson head to toe
above his mother's torso,
her arms shot off by blast

on the way to Damascus.
He conjured the home
of the Caliphs in flames like orange lilies
thrown by an emperor whose religion
was founded on mercy. And a game-

show host from Nebraska, upset
the President of Iraq didn't get
that Israel had a right to defend itself.
(By now the boy's mother
had died.) He started a new thing,

skeletons knifing a king, another
side-saddle on a grey horse
in shafts of a broke-wheeled caboose
overladen with bodies; a lone corpse
floating, swelled belly upwards,

downriver, dogs gnawing the face
of a toddler: plus three-headed Cerberus,
one muzzle searching for fleas,
one head asleep, a third
keeping watch on a black bird

making its nest in red jasmine.
They praised
the painstaking draughtsmanship
in his torn men
dying on wheels, failed rebels

stuck on poles in cassis-coloured sky,
and black feathers on a high
thin horizon from cities on fire;
including I may say Nazareth –
and Bethlehem

where the emperor's pin-up, a.k.a.
the Prince of Peace, was born.
He said that's what I've seen. Yes,
they said, that's what we wanted.
*The Triumph of Death.*

*Ruth Padel*

# AMEN

I dreamt I was a butterfly flying through the air
and knowing nothing of Chuang Tzu,
who carried both pineapple and a grapefruit.
Now, *that* is one mathematical singularity.
The next thing was to envision an alternative to it.

I owed the accidental discovery of mysterious microwaves
to the conjunction of a mirror and an encyclopaedia.
They suffered from a host of maladies, real and imaginary,
which lead to fits of hysteria and frequent disruptions.
The noise was likely to be heard only by the occasional stray caribou.
I was quite alone. So I at once telephoned, saying:

"Dear Jesus, do something.
I do not mean to put the director in a strait jacket,
but precautions have to be taken in the case of freak reincarnation.
Imagine being a hick family or a talking mule.
I'm not sure who first applied the armpit label but this concept is like
a sprawling paradigm of ill-conceived town planning.
I want church in a bar. I want to pass out and hear you say Amen."

He suppressed the idea of laughter,
Preferring to refrigerate it for twenty four hours. He explained:
"The facts of the matter are morally plain, as we have seen repeatedly.
(He was not a traitor, he was a man enlightened, a convert)
You are not lighting a pyre, you are lighting a labyrinth of flames.
One who loves the people can be troubled. Hey, Nice running shoes!"

It's any wonder he's smiling.
However, he did not produce the majority
of brainwashing propaganda movies.
His first love was his most chaotic shoot.
He carried it in his arms to the broken window.
His red flannel shirt lay on the grass.
I once longed to compile its mobile history.
The house burnt like a giant chrysanthemum, all golden.

*Kathryn Parratt*

# THE ASYLUM SEEKER

In 1979
the turquoise veil of Mashad
osmoses into Ealing Green, where
thorny roses acquaint her face
with English concrete.

Gravity thumps to the muck,
new words dangle off people's mouths
too quickly
here, they split into flight.

Feeding crows from a park bench
'For months', she says, 'this is
how we pinch each others stories,
London and I'.

One hand is busy moving
borders
slowly, one at a time.
The body dives from a Babylonian crag
into form.

Capital
cities
coat her temple.

Breadcrumbs
tap the lands
for lucky stars

and fat man behind desk,

that fat man behind desk
has yet
to stamp the future.

*Siavash Pournouri*

# DOWN UNDER

Tourists rise from a king-sized bench,
twenty toes stink of youthful indifference,
the cobbled stones that pave beer gardens
where dreams
punch the dreams
of other would-be artists.

Come watch'em smack themselves,
lure sweetness out of bottles
and nothing else.

Swing by an alley,
where the local bitter spills to form
palettes for a canvas
thick as brick.

Dabbling their shoelaces in urine colours,
visitors come here to paint themselves
frescos and portraits,
hang them on the Southern Cross.

*Siavash Pournouri*

# TO UNICYCLES

I am of a minority who had the chance to get to know you
And I loved our times together
Your seat warmed my thighs

The things we did together, oh!
The half pipes we tried to conquer
The steps on the Southbank

Sometimes, I was mean to you,
I let my anger spill and when I kicked you
I deserved the scratch you gave me back

Ashley, my first love,
you have a special place with me

And now there is Greg
your redness makes me happy

And Mun,
you make me look so tall
Together we make children point

We have worked together for years now, outside when it was cold.

Sometimes I still wave at you
From the bedroom window
And I want to get out and ride

*Sarah Rabone*

# YOU MISSED SOMETHING EARLIER (YOU SAID)

*for Anna*

inside this thing that is not yet a thing (but a certainty
perhaps, you say, nonetheless), inside that

silence.
and seal song. and salt-stamens, that hardened post spray;
found out-of-date in pillow creases at the changing of sheets. or
perhaps they

howl rather than sing. we sand-sank past letters to write names through
        shale-faces -
upturned raw to stub toes on; to blink on contact, eyesight and tide.

we went to wales and fell in love. too simple a story to overcomplicate
with words. so we took them out on a boat and jettisoned letter by
        letter
forgetful acronyms and alphabet. gave the engine a kick and floated for
        days
watched
kelp. selkie-women and welks stick stone-to-stone for life, these underwater fiefdoms.

you wore the crown at night. and starfish-like we matched suckers,
limb-linked and stripped.

now pollen stains white paint.
we wait. watch picture frames tidying dust .
and book an island for the springtime.

*Rowan Rutter*

# THE RAIN-GLASS

Flawless water – blank, like a lens –
lies where it's least expected.
      Your foot sinks through a world
      that's clear as a dream; bell-clear,

water sounds on all sides.
Drains and pipes ring, rinsed
      to a concrete vowel
      of culvert, a gutter's tinny flow –

bright distractions for your ear –
till the world shakes clear
      in collisions of bin-lids and wind-milled trees
      that free

some drop of you,
undressed and new.

*Fiona Sampson*

# DAZZLING, IN OTHER WORDS.

If there is a translation of this,
will it be a feature film, or a radio drama?
How will it capture the garbage we sat through?
The eighty-odd frames of unfurnished backdrops,
until you said, that's enough, now that's enough.
Or did we choose the wrong revolving door,
the endgame & a mouthful of traffic accidents?
One lad performed the brilliant task
and transformed into a stallion.
He's a bit busy at the moment,
& can't be here to accept his trophy.
He doesn't want to make a speech on video.
This will have to do, the crackling vinyl,
does the title denote the correct emotions?
We'll have to get on with it & embrace
the fact that we enjoy all the wrong things.

There is perfect snow on our pave-stones,
Let's hope they stay that way.
Surely it's better to have a few surprises?
I said, watch, time will stop for us,
She said don't try to complicate everything,
you'll be surprised by what we aren't supposed to know.
All we needed was a moment on a bench.
"We're going to the everywhere, I swear."
What a response! and right before
the night was about to get started.
I ask you, then, is it ever safe to make assumptions?
A frantic dollop of this, a cautious dollop of that
Are they happy with the results? Results?
They're upstairs inside a plastic urn, kept safe
by a gang of well-nourished dilettantes,
who love their debates about escape velocity.

*Nima David Seifi*

## THE SADNESS OF POWER LINES, A PLAY

Up-selling playground myths, for
    a pocket of heavy eyes, singing and dialing, the
    eleven strokes of a give or take dilemma. To love
    a person who thought it might pan out.

How much perfume did she need for the fanatic's fire?
How much time did he need for the fanatic's fire?

Bottle-shaped women struggle to breathe,
    side by side, arms linked around the dinner table.
He asks, "What'll happen if we put them on the flame?"

I wanted to take a photograph,
    of that day we shared the famous loaf.
But you had a face like a G chewing a wasp,
    & there were tire-marks all over the place.

I stopped caring once my hair was ruined,
    "Where are your minutes and excuses?" she coughs.
A dusty cabinet lands on her damp palm,
    as we sit quietly in the cul-de-sac.

We had a list of pathbreaking ideas,
    the, you'll get this or that if you do that / sort
It was illegible & I didn't want to eat you,
    but then you weren't ever able to cry.

Is this empathy? Is that a smile?

The toilet is clogged with soggy library cards,
      but she was never one for books.
He stood inside the dreams of guide dogs,
      while the blind pulled faces in the corner.
She says she's sick of praying for what can't be touched:
      "There's six billion, too much to do and feel."
Who is going to write them down,
      when all we have left is a tub of used pens?
This was the danger in not having a plan,
      But then, our tongues were already dead.
Who buries the tongues?

On that note the audience fizzled-out,
      as I pulled over to check your punctures.

*Nima David Seifi*

# FLOOD

The flood will be here soon: in the kitchen.
Its first breach of the back door
Will trickle over the linoleum like silence.
Let it pool under your feet,
Quenching your warm soles in its path to
Lap the skirting board,
Drawing out the floor to a grey mirror.

The house will sink into its rising waters:
A soft skin pierced by table legs and chairs.
An umbrella in the hallway; your cold calves.
Be stolid through this transition:
Feel the rise of slow destruction
Pass you through, as upcast sunlight
Tumbles on your skin like lace.

The flood will climb the stairs with you,
Chasing each apologetic drip that falls down
From your back by slipping onto the next stair.
Reach the bedroom. Rug and paperbacks,
Lifted by the floating tide and muddied
By your filthy carpet stains will rise beside
The loosened plaster of the eiderdown,

As where I was is rinsed way. Your
Wardrobe clothes will crinkle with the wash,
Shirts and trousers floating from their hooks
And scrunching up like muscles.
Your hair is lifted, your neck stroked,
And finally I'll kiss you in the flood,
Devouring your mouth with ageless water.

*Sam Sedgman*

## YOU MEET A POET OF LESS TALENT

You are so seldom drunk in the morning sun,
Awaking from a midsummer night's dream
Allowing a seven o'clock poem to be spun.

But go, listen: hear of the chilly sun beam,
How that guy's working Thursday, Friday, Sat,
Or how Reginald is chilling out in Leam.

He says he used to plan his art projects like that,
Admiration falling for your gifted brown-skinned books
You carry with a smoke and pen to make the covers fat

With words: a scatter-gunned approach to lines resisting looks
From passers-by, mashing up the different signs
Of city life with near-remembered evenings. But how he hooks

You with a glance and hair-tuck, tapping out his lines
In hasty mess like buskers by the statue,
Grinning at the thought that even though it's Indian it rhymes,

And going on with it because there's nothing else to do,
His thoughtless word momentum edging you in silent sound,
A sketch of skin, of body, the morning hours: of "you".

Ignore the action of his pen, scratching out around
The morning dew a lie. It bullies out the night time,
But catches in the weave of poetry the edge of meanings you have found:
The ravages of dusk; slow lies of sunshine.

*Sam Sedgman*

# KALI MA

I was watching a bird take flight over
the dying city, the City of Joy,

when her fuming air clasped my throat,
her fourth arm already black round my belly.

'Do you see freedom *there*, firenghi?
Poet!' she spat in my ear;

at once I could hear
the grate of the crow's slow wing-bones,

scattered eddies of third-hand breath
mourning their climb to the white hot eye.

*Nicola Seth-Smith*

# THE ELITE

It was Vespers: but none of us knew the name of the time
or had heard of its meaning.

We gathered round,
wondering how to save her.

"Water has infinite soothing qualities."
This, from the man who'd sat beneath a mural 'til the lights dimmed.

"But is the infinite soothing?" he winced
and we watched as his eyeballs calcified.

"Maybe we shouldn't let her drink," said the woman who took her first
breath
on hanging a *Munch* above her bed.

"Agreed," said the man beside her.
"I've been taking the stuff for months, and look.

"My skin's so soft from immersion,
I'd be nibbled to death by those fish."

We turned and stared at the fish bowl,
united in accusation.

"Maybe art and love aren't meant for her.
Do we really know what this woman wants?"

"Forget about her. Let's fill up the bowl with a bag of soil
and give them a human burial."

As we debated, she shot up behind us,
choking on soil pouring freely from her.

All knelt at her lap - even the stranger -
with a burning desire for the pile of earth.

But while some of us ate larger handfuls than others,
none of us wept, or were satisfied.

*Nicola Seth-Smith*

# REINVENTION IN A THREE-ACT STRUCTURE

Act One: disown yourself, forget your name,
try silence for a while; resign in twenty-
eight point font, and break your lovers' hearts
in Comic Sans clichés; throw out your clothes/
friends/family/principles (there isn't space
for politics in Reinvention 101,
but if you must, vote Tory [absentee]).

Act Two: the show begins; try on your new
identities, and introduce yourself
with new lies daily; write a fake memoir;
find God, and lose him irrevocably;
combine your latest selves: read Proust in clubs,
and backpack to the mall; then overeat
with anorexia - hit all the trends.

Act Three: the fun is in destruction; pick
a name - Mercedes Rochester will do;
self-actualise through lying, take a stand
on nothing much, and leave bad poetry
behind; wear things you never would, and date
a boy you've never liked; you'll soon regress,
write haiku, drop your placards, tell the truth.

The coda's compromise: pick out a scarf
or two, new shoes; go wild: wear a hat.

*Bethany Startin*

# LETTER IN NOVEMBER

A Cento

I can write the saddest poem of all tonight,
writing this to be as wrong as possible to you.

Look at the light through the windowpane,
those lights that have been burning night and day

the days and the night you were leaving
no one, leaving as a season fades,

leaving the page of the book carelessly open,
gently, like moonlight on a window seat.

Slums, years, have buried you. I would not dare
to rescue the refrain of this song from becoming a dirge.

You want a better story. Who wouldn't? A forest, then.
No asphalt, no rest stops, just a bunch of dead grass

where nothing else matters but the dew and the light,
where nothing, when it happens, is never terrible enough.

*Bethany Startin*

# DARLING SONG

*My darling when she wakes, brings the morning with her,*
she sang to the child in the morning as she woke.
But sometimes darling grouches and wakes in a foul mood,
and sometimes when she's bad, you're so angry you could choke.
*But darling when she wakes, brings the morning with her,*
she sang to the child in the morning as she woke.

*My darling when she rises, causes the sun to rise,*
she sang to the child in the morning as she rose.
But sometimes darling bickers and leads you a merry dance,
and sometimes darling grabs you and leads you by the nose.
*But darling when she rises causes the sun to rise,*
she sang to the child in the morning as she rose.

*My darling does not bicker, my darling doesn't grouch,*
*my darling is my morning, my sunrise, and my song.*
*There are no buts in darling, there's only ever darling,*
*and darling is delight, and darling can't be wrong.*
*So darling wakes and rises, so my darling's born,*
*so darling is for singing, so darling is my song.*

So, lordlings, here's to darlings. We drink to darling's birth,
since darling is to singing, as singing is to voice,
as morning is to waking, as sunrise is to daylight
as kissing is to loving, and joy is to rejoice,
and here's an end to singing this, and here the child is sung
at the morning's high beginning, in the morning sun's own voice.

*George Szirtes*

# FROM THE ARMCHAIR

It was green, it was silent, the rain fell
Without any noise whatsoever and the bed
Lay unmade in the tall room
Where nothing moved throughout the afternoon.
It was late, later than ever, in the time
Before time began. The room was melancholy,
Grown deaf to itself. It was round about four now.
In other rooms chairs and tables
Held their usual conference. All day
It had been raining, and through the window
Fields stretched and gathered themselves for evening.

And then he spoke as if from the armchair,
His voice rising a little before him.
There was a kind of grating sound in him
Which was the sound of rain or furniture.
And then more rain, and then the evening falling.

*George Szirtes*

# SOIL PLAY

We were picking at the soil –
winter heaped on our backs like
a thick fur coat turning all warmth
outward, we were unearthing
bits of old things – the kind of old
that hasn't found the time to rot.

We bathed under-grown, childish fingers,
gloveless with their small, hard nails into
the unturned earth. The floor had grown bobbly,
a fleece worn too long.

I found china, pottery, terracotta, clay, stone, earthenware,
the names of ages and an icecream packet, lost a lot of blue,
steamed and from 1988. All the bits hard and cold.

Carrier bags, a vegetable patch,
the smell of hunting had been
caught and subscribed to the trees –

bird's eyes sat on electric wires, laughing orange arrow beaks
at how we can't remember what they only pretend they can.

In the pig-fat middled, pug-belly
gooseberry bushes – we sit on ground,
filth having dressed us. These separate,
segregated, white, hard, stoned,
torn away pieces that fill
our jars like bug's eyes.

*Cari Thomas*

# SANDWICHES

We've mapped out lives, removed
surprise like you – when you
picked up that knife – it was to cut
bread, make lunch passionately.

                    Dedicated to your task as you unpeeled
                    the plastic sealed packet of ham,
                    stripped from the pig into
           dysfunctional slices. You ripped off

that lettuce as though
it had co-ordinates you needed
for war, stripped its green winged
dignity – your hands adjusted

                    feverishly. You held a babies head
                    in the tomato, fingers barely on
                    that reddened skin and sliced
                    its equator (only to segregate

different parts of its life)
Some you placed face down,
some face up, though both
between bread all the same.

                    You coughed, things tremored and
                    as always your eyes were a mirror
                    — were alive. Slapped your palms
                    on that bread, spread it and lashed on

your butter; lovers, feeling
harmoniously close. This sandwich
took four minutes, thirty five seconds.
Hunger returned after two hours.

                    You picked up the knife as though
                    you could be a killer, a painter,
                    something that had not been
                    cut across the equator.

*Cari Thomas*

# NOVELLA

After Rimbaud's *Roman*

I

You can't be serious when you're twenty-one
-the evenings flare, a rolled joint behind your ear,
Drunk on Wednesdays, university veteran!
You talk in your backyard of us all being queer.

The weed smells great on those June afternoons!
So sweet you could sleep through those exams;
The wind carries laughs – you're humming a tune
Older than you, something about Vietnam.

II

The sky is all yours, you spy it through brambles
Palpitating like grass you would like to caress...
   You think the answer's there to be unscrambled
If only the stars stopped changing their address.

June nights! Twenty-one! Easy to be wasted.
The cheapest wine is the same as any champagne...
You ramble about the Bourdieu you tasted,
Your lips pucker like a socialist campaign.

III

You bildungsroman through books until
You spot some heroin perched on a stool,
With the fruit machine lights pulsing her still
face red, green and blue. You forget the rules.

She calls you a kid when you try to explain
(as her long nails trot gamely on the board)
Why you are superior to her boyfriend,
But she leaves with her glass, looking bored.

IV

You are in love: rented until August!
You are in love. She finds your poems laughable.
Your friends leave, your laundry starts to encrust
When at last, she responds to your madrigal!

That evening, you leave home for the suns
You order a kiss or a ginger beer
You can't be serious when you're twenty-one
And there are summer evenings to premiere.

*Claire Trévien*

# DAFFODILS

Who knew daffodils could grow in a mess?
Socks on my Catullus, hat heaps, wrappers
waiting for my feet to walk on; papers –
too many white sheets, wrinkled and distressed,

some seeking solace under the bed, ha!
There is no sun there, no haven: metal
grips, the carpet's dandruff and excess hair
are all they'll find. They'll cry: "there must be more!"

For sure, old pens with caps lovingly chewed,
that list with names I now – not to be rude –
plain don't need, but outside… Outside is what
They crave. A jungle of glossy weeds sat

with fag ends and cosy corks. Those are their thrills,
for in those somehow grow the daffodils.

*Claire Trévien*

# GHOSTS

All the houses in this city
have ghosts. The shops in Little India
and the stalls in China Town all
full of ghosts. Sometimes you'll see a pickup
full of ghosts, Sri Lankans, Tamils,
making their way to a construction site,
under bridges or in alleys
howling with airconditioning units.
I found a line in one ghost's poem, which read:
*You can't take the kampongs out*
*of the people* and to me it sounded
defiant, but later I learned what it meant.
She was cute; her dad worked
for the government. At night I swim
with the ghosts in the pool by the flats,
their wakes skimming behind their empty shapes.

*George Ttoouli*

# THIS POEM ALL THE TIME

*for HMN*

I'm starting to write a poem
and you're thinking it'll be about
flowers or dead people or a celebration
of the latest coronation in Hungary
but actually it's about a bloke called George
who I tell you is a poet and lecturer,
but you're already distracted
and you're thinking it'll be hard to read
and full of references you might get
but will feel patronised by anyway
and you start thinking about doing a sudoku
and tapping your foot, expecting me to write
about the shepherd Glafkis who fell off a cliff
while picking flowers and would have died
if he hadn't been turned into a dolphin
by a sea nymph who was in love with him
and was later crowned queen of Hungary
but you're bored with thinking about it
and then I surprise you by saying
*this poem is about you I'm writing it for you*
with your butterfly shoes tapping away
and your face behind the paper
and I'm writing about how I would
put a tiara on your head right now
and bring that royal blood up to your cheeks
if only I had one and, sure, this academic bloke
sounds like a bit of a dope but when you get home
you'll be thinking about this poem all the time
because I've been thinking about it for months
on the tube, during the fiesta, or while waiting

for you outside curry houses while you get your coat
and my point is that I've had lots of thinking time
so it should be excellent and when you're done
reading you'll probably think to yourself,
*Yes, now I want to stop reading*
*and do nothing for a long time.*

*George Ttoouli*

# HEADLESS STATE

*for Jules and Ripa*

The bulletin you have been given
design principles and sociological commentary
does nothing to prepare you for the end of day.
Dust trails fin the office air like a rusty car
between fields, a slow presence ploughing
the desk to the window. A scene beyond
the glass draws you back: a peregrine
stutters to the ledge of the facing roof
and tears a pigeon apart. You are
cobwebbed by the sunset's fade upon the eaves,
disembowel in the peregrine's careful talent
for detachment and perfect unity.
For some time, stern silence accepts
the endless fuzzing of a machine.
Even the bodiless chiefs beyond your ken
with their mechanisms to run a state, never this free.

*George Ttoouli*

# A FOLK-SONG FOR EDWARD THOMAS

leaves bursting
beetles climbing
horse-flies humming over an inch of thawing ice

dog's mercury flowering
fieldfares squealing
elms glowing rust-red with flowers in the sun

kingfishers building
water-crickets stirring
flags show a foot above the waters of the brook

chiffchaff singing
hedge-sparrow laying
cuckoo at Wimbledon crying in the oaks

blackbirds building
whitethroats chattering
diving & ascending, peewits seem to creak

herb bennet blossoming
honeysuckle flowering
young whitethroats gaping in the nest

peacock shrieking
swallows twittering
stonechats in the furze on the windy warren-hill

hemlock flowering
blackberry blossoming
stonecrop with mallow on the dry ha-ha wall

teasel plumes purpling
rosehips reddening
yellow lady's bedstraw growing thick on the banks

skylarks skipping
peewits flocking
small insects thronging high up in the twilight air

*Simon Turner*

*All the phrases in this poem, with some minor adjustments for metrical unity, are taken from Edward Thomas's 'A Diary in English Fields and Woods', originally published as part of* The Woodland Life *in 1897.*

*nor in the morning when the rain has stopped*
nor in the coffee shop with the steam congealing
nor underground nor in Wyoming, nowhere &
nowhen, not in the playground or in the fore-
court, nor in the neon streaking the rainy streets
nor in the taxi in the velvet night, & certainly
not in the morning paper or the morning coffee
dregs, dregs of the morning, rain in the morning
rain in the paper too, no not here, no not never
nor in the drawers with the cut-throat scissors
nor in the clouds with the neon congealing
in Wyoming, velvet clouds of nowhen, rain
on the neon streets in some movie of October
nor in my head when the rain comes through
making no stops until Wyoming, clouds congealing
in the coffee, not here, nor there, nor anywhere
nor in the park with the light receding, nor
over the lake as the clouds depart & take the rain
off to Wyoming in the morning, not through the river
& into the trees, nor where angels fear to tread
nor in the temple of the golden pavilion, no no no
nor in the paper taxis melting in the velvet rain
nor in the stain on the bedside table, nor
the flight of birds scared up from the railway tracks,
the city in winter, well you won't find it there,
but in the movie of *Wyoming*? maybe, on fast track
skipping through the footage of trees made of paper
& the velvet streaks of coffee smearing the morning
the nowhen of morning, noplace, neverwhen, cut-throat rain
& clouds of neon & Wyoming receding in the night

*Simon Turner*


*The first line is the last line of Frank O'Hara's 'Poem' ('now the violets are all gone…')*

# TRACES

*for Rochelle*

A zipper of vapour
severs sky from sky,
speaking of the jet just gone;

a feather cleaves
to the seed-bell,
ragged and wind-

shivered, a stray scrap
of the bird who fed there
weeks and weeks ago.

Late June,
and the day's light
blues towards evening,

the white jasmine's
palpable musk
clotting the zesty air,

blackbird and song thrush
gabbing from the holly,
beating the bounds.

A poem remembers:
it's an archive
of the least detail,

less than a feather,
less than vapour, yes,
but something, at least,

I can give you —

*Simon Turner*

# KIRILLOV'S SERENADE

When God died
I passed through the woods by Queen's Court
and sat in the violet
Berkshire dusk. Hawthorns decaying
at my toes and I

whispered to the earth to take me:
cold bells were calling in the silence.
Every autumn, I long for fathers;
and remember witnessing
the prophet raised alone

above a Moscow roundabout
in the snow, marmoreal
as if what he saw displeased
him. I wanted to kiss his eyes,
swallow the icy stone

and reach the living in the dead.
We raced to Lenin's redbrick tomb: aged
soldiers jostled us past the corpse
as if frightened
that we might wake him.

*Jonathan Ware*

# MILL BAY

Stop and listen
to the universes breaking
on each other:

the meeting of
cliff and tide and worlds:
*vibralto* shifts,

fluidity
in everything. The sun erupts
in crystal smoke

and the sky melts
into black from the horizon.
So now I know

for certain how
this might exist beyond me
but in me, breaking

perspective's hold:
and I remember, hot salt
stinging my cheeks

on Mill Bay, aged
five or six, I pushed together
boundaries of sand

that stood cresting
the cold infinite sea, trying
to make it mine.

*Jonathan Ware*

# THE WRESTLER

Waiting on the cliffroad,
muscle brimmed and taut
as a wolftrap's spring:
at Hydra they crowned him
an excess of person,
conqueror of bulls
and terror to the children.
His medal's faded into
saltflecked cataract
and fat swells in his arms
like leavened bread.
He watches, anxious,
hoping for the trundle
of wheels or a bobbed scalp
approaching with the noonday sun.

*Jonathan Ware*

# LOVE TURPENTINE

Turpentine electrifies the air:
I strip out the paints on parchment,
Whitewash out the faces from before
And begin to sketch yours from memory
Of touch. Not looking-glass work of makeup,
Or sycophants. Stroke your texture onto rough,
So that you, through me, can live this parallel life
In art for only us to comprehend and share as muses.

As a poet, you do the same, in your own way, sit behind
Me as I work, mapping my scent and taste in words,
You touch my back and you lean close to smell.
As I scratch my canvas with my bare hand
The linseed oil traps underneath my nails
Even when I twist round to kiss you,
Your face like a skull in my hand,
The oil does not stain your skin.

> The paint is monochrome, like the ink.
> From behind you wrap your legs around my waist,
> Stroke my working arms, furrow your nose
> Into my nape. I twirl and we nose duel,
> Then you turn away to scribble in your book.
> I reach to feel your hair, teasing it
> Through my painted fingertips,
> Squeeze brushes into turps, dab them on old socks.

> When we finish in chorus,
> There'll be no grand unveiling
> Or awkward award ceremony, or prize.
> Jet black portrays us both, in the other's eyes.

*Hilary Watson*

# PARAMETERS

Night sits on the trapdoor to the priesthole
where the sea hides, fervent. In Einstein's
universe, nothing travels faster than light.

A scrambled signal of lantern and torch
plots the shelf's co-ordinates for as far
as I can see, or as far as it is fished.

The news of Jesus' birth could not have been
proclaimed to more than one in two hundred
million million of the known stars.

I ease lugworm onto the barb, threading
the hook's neck, and cast for the parameters
of a seabed that falls and deepens beneath me.

There is something in this string of fishermen,
countable pebbles apart, that a universe
of light years couldn't travel between.

Our common characteristics suggest a mind
that longs, despite the salt-dried face,
to wire itself in to the nerve of God.

*Andrew Webb*

# CONSTRUCTION QUARRY

There is no let up to the beaks
of the squat, limb-necked birds
perching improbably on walls.

London will have its delivery.

Here in the herculean heft to sound
the turned sod of an age, I translate
their song: *fuck, fuck, fuck you*

*Andrew Webb*

# GESTURE

Unlike the murdered father's ghost whose arm
beckons his son to the removed ground of speech

or the hero whose hands reach over a trench
black with sheep's blood to have his mother

prove incorporeal, the bonobo's 'reach up out'
is neither prefixed nor suffixed, knowledge

that promises even so to tell the story of how,
sometime in the last two hundred thousand years,

the mutation of a codon in chromosome seven's
FOXP2 took gesture from the hand to the mouth

releasing - like history from the split-atom – phalanx,
wheel, the larynx from the windpipe's stranglehold.

*Andrew Webb*

*Poultry catcher: the only position*
no one seemed to fill. *Piece-rates.*
and *anti-social hours* but *good prospects,*
*experience not essential.* His mates

took the piss, but Tom was desperate.
*Beggars can't be choosers*
he'd say. *The wheat, the chaff; the men,*
*the boys.* He was *no waster.*

As an animal lover, Tom found
the job of poultry catcher
hard to stomach, but what the hell!
he took his lot, didn't badger

His boss for a rise or hourly rate.
The pay was chicken feed.
Knuckling down to the task in hand,
he did the mercenary deed.

He'd do a tour of the battery farms.
Using the night to disguise
his presence, avoid panic. Into
the selected bird's startled eyes

he'd shine his torch, fixate the thing.
Its ruffled neck outstretched,
he'd bring his hand slowly
round, trying not to retch.

With finger and thumb he'd snap its neck.
He had to get through quite a few
to pay his bills, his student loans.
There was nothing else to do.

When he got laid off, at least
he stopped talking turkey
about *wasters* and *good prospects*
and took his dole gracefully.

*Andrew Webb*

# JOHN BARLEYCORN

Between the cured air and the cauterised land,
he extrudes his skin, gives up his bakelite eyes.

A flute of memory he can't be sure is his own:
how he died and died among the strawed husks,

the crown surround of hill, a fire; above, moons
that bleed and an ox-hide of an oak tree,

its blackbirds, musical boxes unwinding into silence
- melted ears, or desertion, he couldn't be sure.

Only in the limbo of uncertainties
can faith scarify the earth for barleycorn to follow.

*Andrew Webb*

# SUPERPOSITIONS

In twilight pared to the thin cloud
behind the horizon's leafless ash,
there's a section-through of the brain's cortex
or pivoting on its neck, a fossilised archaeopteryx

and despite its oceanful of wave functions
and superpositions, the nanoscopic trap's electron,
the moment it's observed, collapses into one
single wave that peaks on this beach.

This beach, its memory of a third dimension
failing, is a wall wet with plaster
while the blacks of the indistinguishable firs
and branches of the sand dunes' evergreens

suggest the relativity of measured distance,
and warn of the trick my memory for names
will play when tomorrow I'll wake as if
I woke in the place I went to sleep.

*Andrew Webb*

*Worple Press* is an independent publishing house
that specialises in poetry, art and alternative titles.

*Worple Press* can be contacted at:
PO Box 328, Tonbridge, Kent TN9 1WR Tel 01732 368 958
email: theworpleco@aol.com.
website: www.worplepress.co.uk

Trade orders: Central Books, 99 Wallis Road, London E9 5LN
Tel 0845 5489911

## TITLES INCLUDE

*Against Gravity* – **Beverley Brie Brahic**
(A5 Price £8.00  ISBN 1-905208-03-0, pp. 72)

'graceful, sensual, smart'    *Thomas Lux*

*Full Stretch* – **Anthony Wilson**
(Price £10 / 15 Euros  ISBN 1-905208-04-9, pp. 104)

'work shaped by both wit and compassion'    *Mark Robinson*

*Bearings* – **Joseph Woods**
(A5 Price £8.00 / 10 Euros  ISBN 1-905208-00-6, pp. 64)

'his work shows an impressive reach and range'    *Eiléan Ní Chuilleanáin*

*A Ruskin Alphabet* – **Kevin Jackson**
(A6 Price £4.50  ISBN 0-9530947-2-3, pp. 88)

'you may like to consult *A Ruskin Alphabet* by Kevin Jackson, a collection
of facts and opinions on ruskin and Ruskinites, together with a variety of
pithy remarks from the man himself'    *TLS*

*Paths of the Beggarwoman: The Selected Poems of
Marina Tsvetaeva* – **Belinda Cooke**
(A5 Price £12 / 18 Euros  ISBN 978-1-905208-11-1, pp. 144)

'a wonderful book'    *Liam Carson*

'a profound sense of authenticity'    *Joy Hendry*

*Looking In All Directions* – **Peter Kane Dufault**
(A5 Price £10.00  ISBN 0-9530947-5-8, pp. 188)

'Wonderful stuff'   *Ted Hughes*

*The Great Friend and Other Translated Poems* – **Peter Robinson**
(A5 Price £8.00  ISBN 0-9530947-7-4, pp. 75)

Poetry Book Society Recommended Translation

*The Verbals* – **Kevin Jackson in Conversation with Iain Sinclair**
(A5 Price £12.00 / 20 Euros  ISBN 0-9530947-9-0, pp. 148)

'Highly interesting.'   *The Guardian*

'Cultists will be eager to get their hands on it.'   *TLS*

*Stigmata* – **Clive Wilmer**
(A5 Price £10.00 / 15 Euros ISBN 1-905208-01-4, pp. 28)

'a brilliant piece of work which brings honour to our time'
                                                    *Sebastian Barker*

*Buried at Sea* – **Iain Sinclair**
(A5 Price £12.00  ISBN 1-905208-06-5, pp. 104)

'the power of a genuine wizard'   *Michael Moorcock*

*A Suite for Summer* – **John Freeman**
(A5 Price £10.00 / 15 Euros  ISBN 978-1-905208-10-4, pp. 78)

'His poetry re-awakens a sense of wonder in us'   *Kim Taplin*

*To Be in The Same World* – **Peter Kane Dufault**
(A5 Price £10.00 / 15 Euros  $20 ISBN 978-1-905208-07-4, pp. 94)

'as fresh and valuable as ever'   *George Szirtes (Poetry Review)*

*Foraging* – **James Aitchison**
(A5 Price £12.00 / 18 Euros  ISBN 978-1-905208-12-8, pp. 184)

'a properly distanced compassion…and a respect for language'
*Elizabeth Jennings*